Brooke + Dave

W9-CXY-938

ESSENTIALS OF MUSIC

FOR

NEW MUSICIANS

DENNIS K. KIELY

Westfield State College
Westfield, Massachusetts

PRENTICE-HALL, INC., Englewood Cliffs, New Jersey

Library of Congress Cataloging in Publication Data

KIELY, DENNIS K   date
    Essentials of music for new musicians.

    Includes index.
    1. Music—Theory, Elementary.   I. Title.
MT7.K456E8   781   74-23405
ISBN   0-13-286492-4

© 1975 by PRENTICE-HALL, INC.
Englewood Cliffs, New Jersey

All rights reserved. No part of this book
may be reproduced in any form or by any means
without permission in writing from the publisher.

Printed in the United States of America

10   9   8   7   6   5   4   3   2   1

PRENTICE-HALL INTERNATIONAL, INC., LONDON
PRENTICE-HALL OF AUSTRALIA, PTY. LTD., SYDNEY
PRENTICE-HALL OF CANADA, LTD., TORONTO
PRENTICE-HALL OF INDIA PRIVATE LIMITED, NEW DELHI
PRENTICE-HALL OF JAPAN, INC., TOKYO

CONTENTS

chapter 3

RHYTHMIC ORDER   *33*

chapter 4

DEVELOPING RHYTHMIC RESPONSES   *55*

chapter 5

MAJOR SCALES   *76*

chapter 11

PREFACE

This text on music fundamentals has been designed for every individual interested in acquiring skill with the basic elements of music notation, rhythms, scales, key signatures, and intervals. Any significant progress in musical studies is contingent upon a thorough grasp of these fundamentals of music.

In general, the material has been presented on a graduated basis so that each new rudiment follows logically. The exercises found at the end of each chapter provide material that will lead to a practical as well as a theoretical grasp of the various elements involved in the reading, writing, performance, and understanding of music.

Acknowledgment is made to my colleagues, Floyd W. Corson, Donald J. Bastarache, and Lloyd Kenneth Manzer, for their helpful suggestions and to Valerie Ramsey for her assistance in the preparation of the manuscript.

Dennis K. Kiely

TONE

AND

NOTATION

TONE AND NOISE

Tone and noise are quite simply sound. The difference between the two types of sound lies in the nature of the vibrations which are involved. If the vibrations are regular, tone is produced. If the vibrations are irregular, noise is produced. Musical sounds or tones involve a regular series of vibrations which can be measured. The higher tones occur when the vibrations are numerous or fast. The lower tones are the result of a slower or lesser number of vibrations.

A single tone has four elements which create a unique effect in the ears of the listener:

The pitch, which is determined by the number of regular vibrations per second;

The duration or time space in which the vibrations occur (measured by the number of vibrations per second);

The dynamics or amount of energy involved, which generally means the degree of loudness or softness in the tone;

The timbre, which refers to the quality or nature of the tone. Each tone-producing element such as the piano, voice, or other instrument creates its own unique timbre.

PITCH AND NOTATION

A given pitch is an actual musical sound, while a note is a symbol placed on a ladder-like device to indicate the relative highness or lowness of that pitch. As you ascend the ladder, the pitches go up; descending motion indicates lower pitches. All pitches are relative to their position on the ladder. The ladder referred to is called the staff. The staff consists of five horizontal lines with four spaces contained within these lines. In addition, vertical lines are placed at the beginning and at the end:

The staff alone will not be enough to call for specific pitches. A symbol called a clef is added to indicate relative degrees of highness or lowness in pitch.

Pitches ranging from medium to high are notated by the symbol , which is referred to as the treble clef. This symbol is also called the G clef since it is an evolutionary result of an early manuscript form of G. It is interesting to note that the symbol

comes to rest on the second line of the treble staff, thereby assigning the pitch name of G to the second line.

Another symbol is used to indicate pitches ranging from medium to low. The bass clef is a descendant of an early manuscript form of F. The bass clef encloses the fourth line of the bass staff with two dots:

This assigns the pitch name of F to the fourth line of the bass staff. Both of these symbols are useful in learning the pitch names of the various lines and spaces.

MUSICAL ALPHABET

The musical alphabet utilizes seven letters of the twenty-six letters of the alphabet of the English language. These letters are A, B, C, D, E, F, G. Reading from left to right, these letters relate to an ascending order of pitches on the staff. In reverse order, they indicate a descending pattern of pitches on the staff.

Ascending

Descending

It is important to note that the pattern of A to G is repeated once the pitch of G has been reached: A, B, C, D, E, F, G, A, B, C, etc.

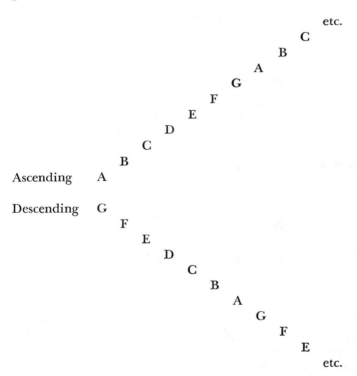

A further example will show a consecutive pattern of pitches arranged in ascending order on the treble staff commencing with the pitch of E rather than A.

LEGER LINES (Ledger Lines)

When there are pitches that are higher or lower than those pre-viously indicated, it becomes necessary to notate them above or below the staff. Lines above or below the staff are called leger lines. Leger lines create the same effect as the line, space, line, space arrangement of the staff. Notes may be added above and below the staff:

Leger lines are added for notes exceeding these ranges:

The bass staff will involve leger lines in the same manner:

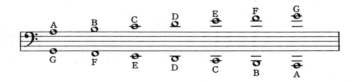

To avoid leger lines above the treble staff, it is customary to use 8^{ve} above the treble staff to indicate pitches actually sounding above the staff although these pitches are written on the staff. These pitches are eight tones higher than the written pitch. The 8^{ve} is an abbreviation meaning an octave (eight tones) higher in this case.

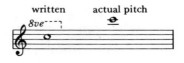

To avoid leger lines below the bass staff, the 8^{ve} is placed below the staff, which calls for a pitch eight tones (octave) below the written note.

If a group of tones is to be notated as 8^{ve}, it is enclosed to show the beginning and end of this notation.

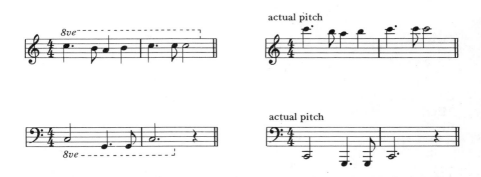

8va is sometimes used instead of 8^{ve}. The result is the same regardless of the spelling.

Another way in which to avoid leger lines is found in the temporary substitution of a different clef sign which will place the notes on the staff. High notes above the bass staff are usually written on the treble staff.

PIANO SONATA, D MAJOR, K.576

Used by permission of Associated Music Publishers, Inc.

GRAND STAFF

A practical device which links the treble and bass staves into one unified whole is the Grand Staff. All pitches from the lowest to the highest can be represented on the Grand Staff. The link between the treble and bass staves is the pitch referred to as Middle C. Middle C is located one leger line below the treble staff and one leger line above the bass staff.

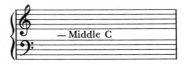

When the treble and bass staves are combined into a Grand Staff, they furnish a continuous series of pitches from lowest to highest with Middle C as the dividing line.

Middle C is also found in the middle of the piano keyboard below the manufacturer's name and generally indicates the division of pitches assigned to the right hand (treble staff) and pitches assigned to the left hand (bass staff).

CHROMATIC SIGNS (Accidentals)

The musical alphabet will generally indicate pitches when placed on the staff. However, a more specific pitch definition is involved when the original alphabet letter indicating a pitch level is not enough to represent the exact number of vibrations per second. Stated differently: every pitch indicated by a letter of the musical alphabet is subject to five possible interpretations:

1. The pitch indicated by the given letter name,
2. The pitch a half step higher,
3. The pitch a half step lower,
4. The pitch a whole step higher,
5. The pitch a whole step lower.

There are five signs used to alter the alphabetical designation of a pitch.

1. The sharp (♯) raises the level of a given pitch one half step.
2. The flat (♭) lowers the level of a given pitch one half step.
3. The cancel or natural (♮) can raise the level of a given pitch if it removes a flat, or it can lower the level of a given pitch if it removes a sharp.
4. The double sharp (♯♯ or ✗) is used to raise a pitch one whole step (two half steps).
5. The double flat (♭♭) will indicate a pitch which has been lowered one whole step (two half steps).

A later study of the piano keyboard should help clarify the function of the sharp (♯), the flat (♭), the cancel (♮), the double sharp (♯♯ or ✗), and the double flat (♭♭).

Exercises

1. Draw a series of G clefs on the staff using the vertical lines.

2. Draw a series of bass clefs on the staff.

3. Write the ascending musical alphabet twice in succession. Begin and end on A.

A B C D E F G A B C D E F G A

4. Write the descending musical alphabet twice in succession. Begin and end on A.

A G F E D C B A G F E D C B A

5. Place the correct pitch names for the lines and spaces on the treble staff.

6. Place the correct pitch names for the spaces and lines above the treble staff.

7. Place the correct pitch names for the spaces and lines below the treble staff.

8. Place the correct pitch names for the spaces and lines above the bass staff.

9.   Place the correct pitch names for the spaces and lines below the bass staff.

10.   Write the actual pitch indicated by the written pitch.

11.   Write the actual pitch indicated by the written pitch.

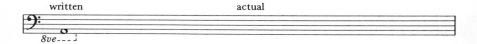

12.   Place the given notes on the correct spaces and lines of the treble staff.

13.   Place the given notes on the correct spaces and lines of the bass staff.

14. Draw a Grand Staff and place the pitch names on each line and space, beginning with Middle C. Include up to two leger lines above the treble staff and two leger lines below the bass staff.

15. Draw the sign that:

    a. Raises a pitch one half step   __#__

    b. Lowers a pitch one half step __♭__

    c. Removes a previous pitch   __♮__

    d. Raises a pitch two half steps __# #__ or __✕__

    e. Lowers a pitch two half steps __♭ ♭__

RHYTHMIC

NOTATION

Musical notation is largely concerned with symbols that are referred to as notes. A note placed on a line or space of the staff will indicate a pitch level. An additional function of a note is to indicate the relative duration of a pitch. Each note has a value that is based upon a series of strong and weak accents which are called the beat. The beat is usually a steady pulse which helps to organize the notes into patterns. The beat also provides a means whereby the numerical value of each note may be determined. The steady tapping of a pencil on a desk is an example of the beat. Tapping one's foot in time to music is another example of the beat.

The beat plays a vital role in the organization of musical sounds which are symbolized by notes. Notes appear as a combination of open ovals (·ᴑ) or filled-in ovals (●) with stems attached. Flags, beams, ties, and dots are added to decrease or increase the value of the notes. These note parts are identified below.

BASIC NOTES

The basic notes used in music notation are:

        o   =   whole note

        ♩   =   half note

        ♩   =   quarter note

        ♪   =   eighth note

        ♬   =   sixteenth note

        ♬   =   thirty-second note

UNCOMMON NOTES

The double whole note ‖o‖ found in Renaissance music is equal to eight quarter notes or four half notes. The sixty-fourth note ♬ is found infrequently.

NOTE RELATIONSHIPS

Table I shows the normal relationships through the divisions and subdivisions of the whole note. The division of the whole note in the table is by two and the subdivisions are by 4, 8, 16, and 32. The name of each note is actually derived from its relationship to the whole note.

The assignment of a value of four beats to the whole note will show the divisions and subdivisions for each note. The assignment of four beats to the whole note is not an arbitrary choice since that is the common value of the whole note. However, a later study of meter signatures will reveal occasions where the value of the whole note is not four beats.

TABLE I: NOTE RELATIONSHIPS

		Total
Whole note	𝐨	= 4

Half note

= 4

Quarter note

= 4

Eighth note

$\frac{1}{2}$ + $\frac{1}{2}$ + $\frac{1}{2}$ + $\frac{1}{2}$ + $\frac{1}{2}$ + $\frac{1}{2}$ + $\frac{1}{2}$ + $\frac{1}{2}$ = 4

Sixteenth note

$\frac{1}{4}$ + $\frac{1}{4}$ + $\frac{1}{4}$ + $\frac{1}{4}$ etc.   = 4

Thirty-second note

$\frac{1}{8}$ + $\frac{1}{8}$ + $\frac{1}{8}$ + $\frac{1}{8}$ etc.   = 4

* Eighth notes joined by a beam. See section under Flags and Beams.

TIES AND DOTS

The duration of any note may be extended by a curved line (tie) connecting two or more note heads. The tie can only be used to connect note heads placed on the same line or space. The duration of the pitch is extended for the total value of all the connected notes. Ties are placed on the opposite side of the note head from the stem.

A dot placed after a note will receive half the value of the note it follows. The undotted whole note will continue to receive four beats. The extended value created by the addition of the dot becomes apparent when a numerical value is assigned.

$$\mathbf{o} \cdot \; = \; \mathbf{o} \; + \; \text{♩} $$
$$4 + 2 \qquad 4 \quad + \quad 2$$

$$\text{♩} \cdot \; = \; \text{♩} \; + \; \text{♩}$$
$$2 + 1 \qquad 2 \quad + \quad 1$$

$$\text{♩} \cdot \; = \; \text{♩} \; + \; \text{♪}$$
$$1 + \tfrac{1}{2} \qquad 1 \quad + \quad \tfrac{1}{2}$$

$$\text{♪} \cdot \; = \; \text{♪} \; + \; \text{♫}$$
$$\tfrac{1}{2} + \tfrac{1}{4} \qquad \tfrac{1}{2} \quad + \quad \tfrac{1}{4}$$

$$\text{♫} \cdot \; = \; \text{♫} \; + \; \text{♬}$$
$$\tfrac{1}{4} + \tfrac{1}{8} \qquad \tfrac{1}{4} \quad + \quad \tfrac{1}{8}$$

Dots added to notes on lines are placed on the next space above the note head. Dots added to notes in spaces should be placed directly beside the note head.

On occasion, a double dotted note is encountered. The value of the second dot is one half that of the first dot.

$$𝅝.. = 𝅝 + 𝅗𝅥 + 𝅘𝅥$$
$$4 + 2 + 1 \quad 4 \quad + \quad 2 \quad + \quad 1$$

$$𝅗𝅥.. = 𝅗𝅥 + 𝅘𝅥 + 𝅘𝅥𝅮$$
$$2 + 1 + \tfrac{1}{2} \quad 2 \quad + \quad 1 \quad + \quad \tfrac{1}{2}$$

$$𝅘𝅥.. = 𝅘𝅥 + 𝅘𝅥𝅮 + 𝅘𝅥𝅯$$
$$1 + \tfrac{1}{2} + \tfrac{1}{4} \quad 1 \quad + \quad \tfrac{1}{2} \quad + \quad \tfrac{1}{4}$$

$$𝅘𝅥𝅮.. = 𝅘𝅥𝅮 + 𝅘𝅥𝅯 + 𝅘𝅥𝅰$$
$$\tfrac{1}{2} + \tfrac{1}{4} + \tfrac{1}{8} \quad \tfrac{1}{2} \quad + \quad \tfrac{1}{4} \quad + \quad \tfrac{1}{8}$$

Dotted notes provide further divisions and subdivisions of rhythmic symbols. Divisions and multiples by three, as well as by two, are now possible. Divisions of a dotted whole note by two will result in the first division of the dotted whole note into two dotted half notes.

$$𝅗𝅥. \quad 𝅗𝅥. = 𝅝.$$
$$3 \quad + \quad 3 \quad = \quad 6$$

Division of the dotted whole note by three will produce three un-dotted half notes.

$$𝅗𝅥 \quad 𝅗𝅥 \quad 𝅗𝅥 = 𝅝.$$
$$2 + 2 + 2 \quad = \quad 6$$

Assigning the common value of four beats to the whole note and half that value (two beats) to the dot will result in a dotted whole note worth six beats.

$$𝅝.$$
$$4 + 2 = 6$$

Division by two: $𝅗𝅥. \quad 𝅗𝅥.$
$$3 + 3 = 6$$

Division by three: $𝅗𝅥 \quad 𝅗𝅥 \quad 𝅗𝅥$
$$2 + 2 + 2 = 6$$

STEM DIRECTION

Stems of notes lying on and above the third line of the staff are drawn downward; those notes placed below the third line have their stems pointing upward. The stems which point upward are drawn from the right side of the note head; downward pointing stems are drawn from the left side. In general, the major portion of the stem would be on the staff.

A single stem attached to two or more notes should be drawn in the correct direction for the note head farthest from the third line. If the highest and lowest notes are equidistant from the third line, the downward direction is preferred.

FLAGS AND BEAMS

Flags added to stems are always drawn on the right side regardless of stem direction.

When the flags are joined, the straight lines which join them are called beams, or sometimes ligatures. Beams replace individual flags and provide groups of two or more adjacent flagged notes.

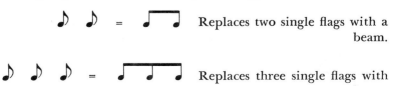

Replaces two single flags with a beam.

Replaces three single flags with a beam.

♪ ♪ ♪ ♪ = ♫♫♫♫   Replaces four double flags with
double beams.

Beams may be used to connect flagged notes of different duration, i.e., notes with varying numbers of flags.

♪   ♪♪ = ♩   ♪♪

♪♪   ♪ = ♫   ♩

Flagged notes of different pitches may also be beamed together. The slant of the beam should follow the general contour of the pitches involved. An alteration in stem direction sometimes may be needed when connecting notes of different pitch. If the majority of the notes lie on or above the third line, the stems point downward; if the pitches mainly lie below the third line, the stems point upward. When there is a question as to the proper direction of the stems, the downward direction is preferred.

Common practice favors flags which are joined although the separation of the flagged notes helps in the reading of vocal music which involves the separation of syllables in the text.

I'm just a   poor way-far-ing strang-er, A trav-'ling through this world of   woe;

RESTS

Music contains measured silence as well as measured sound. The duration of silence is represented by musical symbols called rests. Each note has a corresponding rest. The numerical value of each rest is the same as the value of the related note.

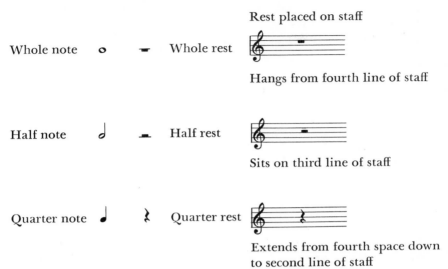

Rests which are the equivalent of flagged notes have hooks that must agree in number with the number of flags on the corresponding notes.

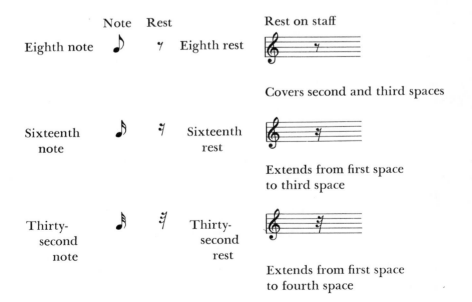

Rests are related in exactly the same way as their corresponding notes. Table II illustrates rest relationships. The whole rest receives four beats, with the divisions and subdivisions receiving the same values as their corresponding notes.

TABLE II: REST RELATIONSHIPS

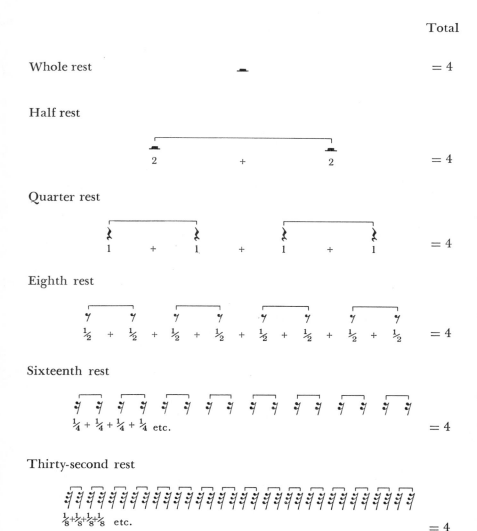

Total

Whole rest   = 4

Half rest

2   +   2   = 4

Quarter rest

1   +   1   +   1   +   1   = 4

Eighth rest

½ + ½ + ½ + ½ + ½ + ½ + ½ + ½   = 4

Sixteenth rest

¼ + ¼ + ¼ + ¼ etc.   = 4

Thirty-second rest

⅛+⅛+⅛+⅛ etc.   = 4

Dotted Rests

Ties are never used to connect rests. However, the duration of a rest may be extended by a dot. A dot increases the length of a rest in the same way a dot increases the length of a note.

Total

$$\blacktriangledown\!\cdot \;=\; \blacktriangledown \;+\; \blacksquare$$
$$4 + 2 \qquad\quad 4 \;\; + \;\; 2 \quad = 6$$

$$\blacksquare\!\cdot \;=\; \blacksquare \;+\; \xi$$
$$2 + 1 \qquad\quad 2 \;\; + \;\; 1 \quad = 3$$

$$\xi\!\cdot \;=\; \xi \;+\; \gamma$$
$$1 + \tfrac{1}{2} \qquad 1 \;\; + \;\; \tfrac{1}{2} \quad = 1\tfrac{1}{2}$$

$$\gamma\!\cdot \;=\; \gamma \;+\; \gamma$$
$$\tfrac{1}{2} + \tfrac{1}{4} \qquad \tfrac{1}{2} \;\; + \;\; \tfrac{1}{4} \quad = \tfrac{3}{4}$$

Rests may be double-dotted; however, they are not frequently encountered. The second dot will receive half the value of the previous dot.

$$\blacktriangledown\!\cdot\cdot$$
$$4 + 2 + 1 \quad = 7$$

$$\blacksquare\!\cdot\cdot$$
$$2 + 1 + \tfrac{1}{2} \quad = 3\tfrac{1}{2}$$

$$\xi\!\cdot\cdot$$
$$1 + \tfrac{1}{2} + \tfrac{1}{4} \quad = 1\tfrac{3}{4}$$

$$\gamma\!\cdot\cdot$$
$$\tfrac{1}{2} + \tfrac{1}{4} + \tfrac{1}{8} \quad = \tfrac{7}{8}$$

IRREGULAR NOTE RELATIONSHIPS

The relationship of notes and rests may change from the normal divisions and subdivisions shown in Tables I and II when a curved line and an Arabic figure are used to enclose a certain number of notes and/or rests.

The most frequent alterations of mathematical relationships are the triplet and duplet. The triplet will be recognized by the curved line with the figure 3 (*3*   ). If a beam is used to connect flagged notes, the curved line is often omitted. However, the figure 3 must be present to indicate a triplet.

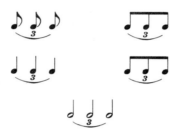

The triplet is always equal to two similar notes of equal value (without the curved line or figure 3). The following example will show various single notes with a value of one beat each dividing into halves and thirds. Attention is drawn to the fact that various notes in addition to the quarter note may be assigned a value of one beat. This variance will be explained in the section on meter signatures.

Single Note Equivalency   *Two Symbols of Equal Value*   *Triplet*

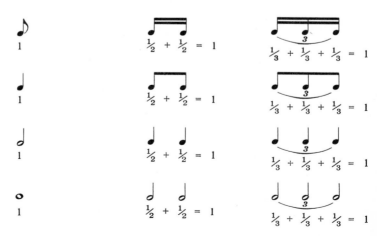

Notice that each triplet is equal to one beat, while the single note alone is equal to one beat. According to Table I, three eighth notes would be the equivalent of one and one-half beats. The table shows the normal division of the quarter note into two eighth notes, not three. The triplet sign now divides the quarter note into equal thirds, i.e., three eighth notes. Study the other examples.

On occasion, rests are included within the triplet. This does not change the mathematical equivalency within the triplet. Each of the following examples contains a rest. Notice that each portion of the triplet is an equal division in thirds. Adding the appropriate rest, the curved line, and the figure 3 to the notes in column two produces a triplet.

Single Note Equivalency   *Two Symbols of Equal Value*   *Triplet*

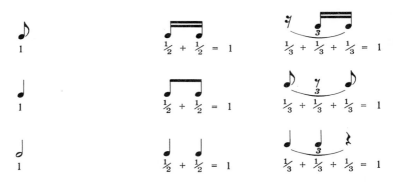

Triplets may consist of unequal notes and/or rests in numerous combinations. Shown below are examples of triplets made up of unequal notes, or notes and rests combined.

Single Note Equivalency   *Two Symbols of Unequal Value*   *Triplet*

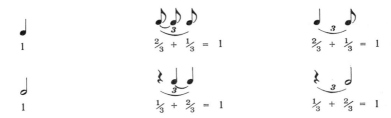

A duplet is a group of two notes which has the equivalency of three equal notes. The duplet is recognized in a manner similar to the triplet; a curved line is used with an Arabic figure 2. On occasion, the curved line is omitted, but the Arabic figure 2 must be present.

Examples of the more frequently encountered duplets are shown below. Reducing by one the notes in column two and drawing a curved line and figure 2 will create the duplet.

Single Note Equivalency   *Three Notes of Equal Value*   *Duplet*

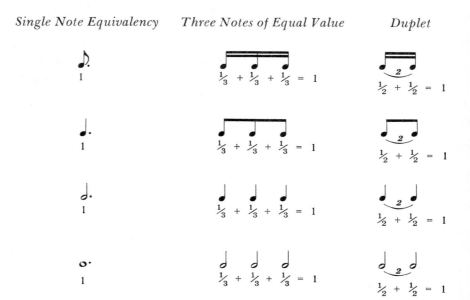

In brief, the duplet or triplet will use the same note or rest, but the number used will be one more or one less, depending on which rhythmic division is needed.

Other mathematical relationships are possible: quadruplets, quintuplets, sextuplets, etc.; however, these are left to a more advanced study of rhythm.

Exercises

1. Identify the note parts.

    ♪.

2. List the basic notes used in music notation in descending order.

3. Draw two uncommon notes and identify them.

4. Draw a table showing the divisions and subdivisions of the whole note, which is worth four beats. Show the correct number of beats in each instance.

5. Using ties and dots, show the equivalents of:

𝅝 + 𝅗𝅥
4 + 2

𝅗𝅥 + 𝅘𝅥
2 + 1

𝅘𝅥 + 𝅘𝅥𝅮
1 + ½

𝅘𝅥𝅮 + 𝅘𝅥𝅮
½ + ¼

6.   Attach stems to these note heads.

a.

b.

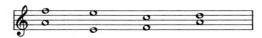

c.

7.   a. Draw single flags on the first pair, then beams on the second pair of note heads.

b. Draw double flags, then beams on each group of four note heads.

c. Beam:

One eighth note and two sixteenth notes

Two sixteenth notes followed by one eighth note

8.   Beam these notes.

9.   Draw on the staff the equivalent rests for:

10. Draw a table of rest relationships based on a numerical value of four beats for the whole rest.

11.   Using a single rest and a dot show the equivalency of:

a.

━   +   ▬   =
4   2

b.

▬   +   ⌇   =
2   1

c.

⌇   +   ❼   =
1   ½

d.

❼   +   ❼   =
½   ¼

12.   Give the divisions by two notes and by three notes for the following single notes.

Single Note Equivalency   *Two Equal Notes*   *Three Equal Notes*

13.   Show the triplet as two notes of unequal value based on:

Single Note Equivalency   *Two Unequal Notes*

14. Write three notes of equal value followed by a duplet for each single note equivalency.

Single Note Equivalency	Three Equal Notes	Duplet
♪.		
♩.		
𝅗𝅥.		
𝅝.		

15. Use one rest in the following triplets.

Single Note Equivalency	Triplet with a Rest
♪	
♩	
𝅗𝅥	

16. Use one rest in the following duplets.

Single Note Equivalency	Duplet with Rest
♪.	
♩.	
𝅗𝅥.	
𝅝.	

17.   On the pitch of A above Middle C, sing the following rhythms using "ta" as a syllable while tapping or clapping the beat. The combinations of rhythms are grouped in four-beat units.

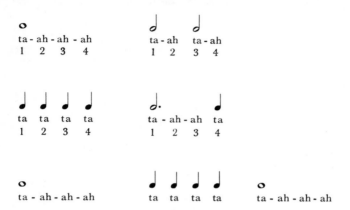

𝅝
ta - ah - ah - ah
1   2   3   4

𝅗𝅥   𝅗𝅥
ta - ah   ta - ah
1   2   3   4

♩ ♩ ♩ ♩
ta ta ta ta
1   2   3   4

𝅗𝅥.   ♩
ta - ah - ah   ta
1   2   3   4

𝅝
ta - ah - ah - ah

♩ ♩ ♩ ♩
ta ta ta ta

𝅝
ta - ah - ah - ah

When rests occur, whisper the word "rest" and continue to tap or clap the beat.

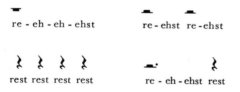

▬
re - eh - eh - ehst

▬   ▬
re - ehst   re - ehst

𝄽 𝄽 𝄽 𝄽
rest rest rest rest

▬.   𝄽
re - eh - ehst   rest

18.   Follow the same procedure for these rhythmical combinations:

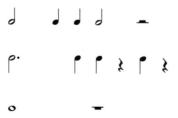

𝅗𝅥   ♩ ♩ 𝅗𝅥   ▬

♩.   ♩ ♩ 𝄽 ♩ 𝄽

𝅝   ▬

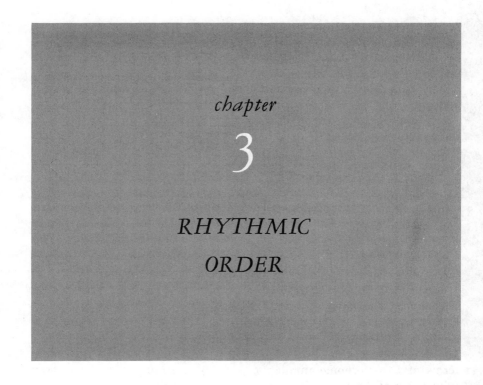

chapter

3

RHYTHMIC

ORDER

Rhythm is the element of music which consists of sounds and silences in various durations. Rhythm moves through time. The symbols indicating duration were identified in the previous chapter. A note placed on a particular line or space of the staff calls for a specific pitch. It also indicates the length of time that the pitch is to be held. In addition, various combinations of notes arranged in patterns with definite accents produce rhythm which, in essence, is the motion of music.

The organization of rhythmic patterns involves basic beats, bar lines, measures, metric groups, simple and compound meter signatures, irregular meter signatures, and tempo. These elements are presented individually so that their specific functions may be analyzed.

BEAT

Previous mention has been made of the vital importance of the beat. More specifically, the basic control for the rhythmic patterns is a continuous and regular pulsation or steady beat. The pulsation of music may be likened to the heartbeat, the ticking of a clock, or certain physical activities, such as walking or running. Often we are motivated to respond to the steady beat of music by tapping our feet or moving our hands, particularly to march music or music that is appropriate for dancing.

The pulsations or beats are equally spaced and of equal duration, but of unequal strength. In a continuous flow of steady beats, certain beats are felt to be stressed while others are not. Some beats are strong (S) and some beats are weak (w). By means of these stresses or accents, regularly recurring steady beats group themselves into metric patterns of twos or threes or combinations thereof. These pulsations falling into patterns of strong and weak beats provide the framework for rhythmic coherence in music.

TEMPO

The speed of the steady beat determines the precise length of the unit of beat. The rate of speed at which the steady beat moves is known as the *tempo* of music. Tempo indications are frequently found at the beginning of a composition over the first staff. The marking may be in terms of a metronome number (♩ = 60), meaning that the quarter note moves at the rate of 60 beats (quarter notes) per minute. The higher the number, the faster the speed. Other tempo markings may be words or phrases in Italian, German, French, or English indicating various degrees of speed.

BAR LINES AND MEASURES

Vertical lines which separate various groups of notes are called bar lines. Bar lines aid in reading rhythmic notation, indicating the strongest accents or beats. The strongest beat is usually the first beat after the bar line. Usually the last beat in each pattern is a weak beat. The time space between any two bar lines is called a measure.

The organization of steady beats into strong and weak pulses through bar lines and measures helps to establish the meter of music.

In addition to single bar lines which indicate measures, there are other combinations of vertical lines found on the staff. The double bar line is found at the end of a section of music or may even mark the end of a composition.

The repetition of a complete section is indicated by two double lines with dots which enclose the section to be repeated.

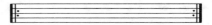

The repetition of a section is sometimes found with only one double bar and dots at the end of a section. That section is also repeated.

Another aspect of repetition using the double bar involves first and second endings. The repetition sign is enclosed in a bracket with the figure 1. The notes within this bracket are performed the first time, but after the repetition of the section, the first ending is skipped and the second ending closes the section or continues to a new section.

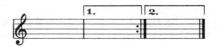

METER

Meter may be considered duple, triple, or quadruple according to the number of strong (S) beats and weak (w) beats contained within each pattern. A pattern which contains one strong beat followed by a weak beat is known as a duple meter.

Duple: Groups of two

A pattern with one strong beat followed by two weak beats is a triple meter.

Triple: Groups of three

A pattern which contains four beats—the first one a strong beat, the third not as strong (a secondary stress), and the second and fourth beats weak—is a quadruple meter.

Quadruple: Groups of four

Other less common groupings will be mentioned later.

The steady beat is temporarily represented here by a quarter note. The note which represents the steady beat is called the *unit of beat*. Any one of the notes found in the Table of Note Relationships in Chapter 2 may represent the unit of beat. However, the quarter note, the half note, the eighth note, the dotted quarter note, and the dotted half note are the most common. If the quarter note is selected, then all other notes are of a precise length in direct relation to it—either as multiples, divisions, or subdivisions of the quarter note.

Meter Signatures—Simple

The metric organization of music is indicated by a meter signature. The two figures which are found at the beginning of a composition or at various sections represent the meter. There is no line between the two figures. Meter signatures are also referred to as time signatures. The upper figure of the meter signature determines the number of beats in each measure. The lower figure identifies the note which will be the unit of beat.

Meters with 2, 3, or 4 as the upper figure are referred to as simple meter signatures. Some of the more common meter signatures are shown in Table III. Note that the unit of beat in each of the following meters is an undotted note. Simple meters are meters which normally divide, subdivide, and multiply by two.

Two simple meter signatures which are not written with numbers but are indicated through symbols are C and ¢ . The C (referred to as *common time*) is another way of expressing $\frac{4}{4}$ meter. The ¢ (referred to as *cut time* or *alla breve*) is the symbol for $\frac{4}{4}$ meter. Actually, $\frac{2}{2}$ meter may be thought of as a fast $\frac{4}{4}$ meter. The increase in speed reduces the value of the quarter note to one half of a beat.

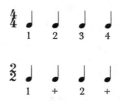

The half note becomes the unit of beat in $\frac{2}{2}$ meter and the quarter note becomes the first division of the beat.

Table IV presents the more common note values found in simple meters. Remember that the unit of beat is always determined by the lower figure in the meter signature.

Meter Signatures—Compound

A simple way in which to identify a compound meter is to use a formula:

If three will go into the upper figure of the meter signature more than once equally, the meter is compound.

For example: $\frac{6}{8}$ meter—three goes into six more than once equally; the meter is compound. Thus, the upper figure of the meter signature will indicate a compound meter if it is a 6, 9, or 12.

The lower figure of the compound meter signature indicates which

Table III: Simple Meters

Signature	Unit of Beat	First Division of Beat	Number of Beats in Each Group	Accents	Type of Meter
$\frac{2}{4}$	♩	♫	2	Sw	Duple
$\frac{3}{4}$	♩	♫	3	Sww	Triple
$\frac{4}{4}$	♩	♫	4	Swsw	Quadruple
$\frac{2}{8}$	♪	♬	2	Sw	Duple
$\frac{3}{8}$	♪	♬	3	Sww	Triple
$\frac{4}{8}$	♪	♬	4	Swsw	Quadruple
$\frac{2}{2}$	𝅗𝅥	♩ ♩	2	Sw	Duple
$\frac{3}{2}$	𝅗𝅥	♩ ♩	3	Sww	Triple
$\frac{4}{2}$	𝅗𝅥	♩ ♩	4	Swsw	Quadruple

TABLE IV: NOTE VALUES IN SIMPLE METER

Meter	Four Beats	Three Beats	Two Beats	One Beat	Half a Beat	Third of a Beat (⅓ each note)	Quarter of a Beat	Eighth of a Beat
2/4			𝅗𝅥	♩	♪	triplet of eighths	♬	thirty-second
3/4		𝅗𝅥.	𝅗𝅥	♩	♪	triplet of eighths	♬	thirty-second
4/4 or C	o	𝅗𝅥.	𝅗𝅥	♩	♪	triplet of eighths	♬	thirty-second
2/2 or ¢			o	𝅗𝅥	♩	triplet of quarters	♪	thirty-second
3/2		o.	o	𝅗𝅥	♩	triplet of quarters	♪	thirty-second
4/2	o‖	o.	o	𝅗𝅥	♩	triplet of quarters	♪	thirty-second
2/8			𝅘𝅥𝅮	♪	♬	triplet of sixteenths	thirty-second	
3/8		♩.	𝅘𝅥𝅮	♪	♬	triplet of sixteenths	thirty-second	
4/8	𝅗𝅥	♩.	𝅘𝅥𝅮	♪	♬	triplet of sixteenths	thirty-second	

note will receive one beat. An 8 on the bottom signifies an eighth note as receiving one beat. $\frac{6}{8}$ meter performed slowly will use the eighth note as the unit of beat. Usually $\frac{6}{8}$ is performed rather rapidly with strong accents on the first and fourth beats.

Note that 1 and 4 are printed larger that 2, 3, 5, and 6. This is done to indicate a basic rapid beat pattern of two beats rather than six.

To speed up a $\frac{6}{8}$ meter we may count faster, accenting 1 and 4,

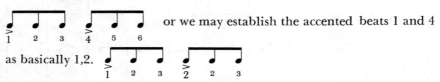 or we may establish the accented beats 1 and 4

as basically 1,2.

If we wish to establish a fast $\frac{6}{8}$ meter of two beats per measure, we can multiply the basic unit of beat (♪) by three, and thereby establish the dotted quarter note as the fast unit of beat in $\frac{6}{8}$ meter.

If each eighth note is worth one beat in a slow   , a quarter note will be worth two beats and the dotted quarter will be worth three beats.

Slow $\frac{6}{8}$ ♪ = 1   ♩ = 2   ♩. = 3

By utilizing the dotted quarter note (♩.) as the unit of beat, we merely combine six beats into a basic beat pattern of two beats per measure and use a larger note value (♩.) as the unit of beat. The two-beat pattern still retains the original feeling for two groups of three found in the slow $\frac{6}{8}$.

Slow $\frac{6}{8}$ 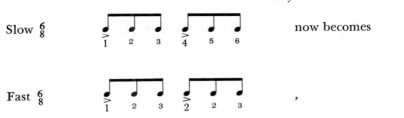 now becomes

Fast $\frac{6}{8}$,

or with the dotted quarter note as the unit of beat:

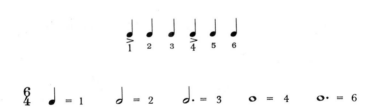

In the fast $\frac{6}{8}$ the three eighth notes ♪♪♪ are considered to be the first division of the dotted quarter note (♩.), which is now the unit of beat.

The same procedure is involved with a $\frac{6}{4}$ meter. Here the quarter note is indicated as the unit of beat:

$\frac{6}{4}$ ♩ = 1   ♩ = 2   ♩. = 3   o = 4   o· = 6

If we wish to establish a fast $\frac{6}{4}$ meter of two beats per measure, we can multiply the basic unit of beat (♩) by three: ♩ ♩ ♩ = ♩.
This will establish the dotted half note as the fast unit of beat in $\frac{6}{4}$ meter. By utilizing the dotted half note as the unit of beat the original six-beat pattern is combined into a basic beat pattern of two beats per measure. Again, the two-beat pattern retains the feeling for two groups of three found in the slow .

Slow $\frac{6}{4}$  now becomes

Fast $\overset{6}{4}$ ♩ ♩ ♩ ♩ ♩ ♩

$\overset{>}{1}$ 2 3 $\overset{>}{2}$ 2 3

or with the dotted half note as the unit of beat:

$\overset{>}{\underset{1}{\text{♩.}}}$ 2 3 $\overset{>}{\underset{2}{\text{♩.}}}$ 2 3

In the fast $\overset{6}{4}$ the three quarter notes ♩ ♩ ♩ are considered to be the first division of the dotted half note (♩.), which is now the unit of beat.

Mathematically, there is no inconsistency in interpreting a $\overset{6}{8}$ meter as six beats to a measure with the eighth note receiving one beat. The major distinction lies in the fact that only rarely does one *feel* six beats per measure in a $\overset{6}{8}$ or $\overset{6}{4}$ meter. Except in music that is very slow in speed, the feeling for the pulse reduces to two steady beats in each measure.

The following tables show the patterns of accents using the un-dotted note as the unit of beat and the dotted note as the unit of beat.

TABLE V: PATTERNS OF ACCENTS (UNDOTTED NOTES)

	Meter	Undotted Unit of beat	Accents
Duple Groups of two	$\overset{2}{4}$	♩	♩ ♩ S w
	$\overset{2}{2}$ ¢	♩	♩ ♩ S w
Triple Groups of three	$\overset{3}{4}$	♩	♩ ♩ ♩ S w w
Quadruple Groups of four	$\overset{4}{4}$ C	♩	♩ ♩ ♩ ♩ S w s w

TABLE VI: PATTERNS OF ACCENTS (DOTTED NOTES)

	Meter	Dotted Unit of beat	Accents
Duple Groups of two	6 8	♩.	♩. ♩. S w
	6 4	𝅗𝅥.	𝅗𝅥. 𝅗𝅥. S w
Triple Groups of three	9 8	♩.	♩. ♩. ♩. S w w
	9 4	𝅗𝅥.	𝅗𝅥. 𝅗𝅥. 𝅗𝅥. S w w
Quadruple Groups of four	12 8	♩.	♩. ♩. ♩. ♩. S w s w
	12 4	𝅗𝅥.	𝅗𝅥. 𝅗𝅥. 𝅗𝅥. 𝅗𝅥. S w s w

Beat Division in Compound Meters

The manner in which the beat divides and subdivides is important in understanding the difference between a simple and a compound meter. When the undotted note is selected, the beat divides and subdivides into two and four, respectively.

Simple Meter

♩　　Beat

♫　　Division of beat

♬♬　　Subdivision of beat

When the dotted note is the unit of beat, the division and subdivision is into three and six.

Compound Meter

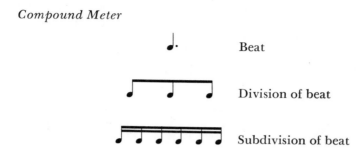

The normal division of the unit of beat in compound meter is by three. Table VII shows the first division of the beat in various compound meters.

Tables VIII and IX which follow present the common note values found in both the slow and fast compound meters. Comparable rest values would apply in the same way. The one exception to note is that rests are grouped together, rather than tied together, to provide the necessary beats of silence. Dots instead of ties are added to rests to increase their value.

TABLE VII: COMPOUND METERS

Signature	Unit of Beat	First Division of Beat	Number of Beats in Each Measure	Accents	Type of Meter
6/8	♩.	(♪♪♪)	2	Sw	Duple
9/8	♩.	(♪♪♪)	3	Sww	Triple
12/8	♩.	(♪♪♪)	4	Swsw	Quadruple
6/4	♩.	(♩♩♩)	2	Sw	Duple
9/4	♩.	(♩♩♩)	3	Sww	Triple

TABLE VIII: COMMON NOTE VALUES IN SLOW COMPOUND METER

Meter	Twelve Beats	Nine Beats	Six Beats	Five Beats	Three Beats	Two Beats	One Beat	One Half Beat
6 / 8			♩.		♩.	♩	♪	♪
9 / 8		♩.·♪	♩.	♩.·♪	♩.	♩	♪	♪
12 / 8	♩.	♩.·♪	♩.	♩.·♪	♩.	♩	♪	♪
6 / 4			♩		♩	♩	♩	♪
9 / 4		♩·♪	♩	♩·♪	♩	♩	♩	♪
12 / 4	♩·♩	♩·♪	♩	♩·♪	♩	♩	♩	♪

46

TABLE IX: COMMON NOTE VALUES IN FAST COMPOUND METER

Meter	Four Beats	Three Beats	Two Beats	One Beat	Third of a Beat (First Division)
$\frac{6}{8}$			𝅗𝅥.	♪.	♪
$\frac{9}{8}$		𝅗𝅥.⌒♪	𝅗𝅥.	♪.	♪
$\frac{12}{8}$	𝅗𝅥.	𝅗𝅥.⌒♪	𝅗𝅥.	♪.	♪
$\frac{6}{4}$			𝅗𝅥	𝅘𝅥.	𝅘𝅥
$\frac{9}{4}$		𝅗𝅥.⌒𝅘𝅥	𝅗𝅥	𝅘𝅥.	𝅘𝅥
$\frac{12}{4}$	𝅗𝅥.⌒𝅗𝅥	𝅗𝅥.⌒𝅘𝅥	𝅗𝅥	𝅘𝅥.	𝅘𝅥

47

Irregular Meters

There are some meter signatures which have not been mentioned thus far. Meters such as $\frac{5}{4}$, $\frac{5}{8}$, and $\frac{7}{8}$ are not as uncommon today as they were a few years ago. In essence, these signatures are combinations of meters discussed earlier. A meter of 5 beats is generally a combination of a 2 plus 3, or the reverse, a 3 plus 2.

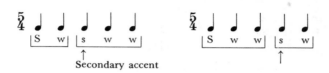

A meter of 7 beats may break into a 3 plus 4, a 4 plus 3, a 2 plus 2 plus 3, or a 3 plus 2 plus 2.

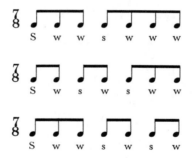

Exercises

1. In the following exercise give the note for the unit of beat, the first division of the beat, and the strong (S) (s) and weak (w) accents.

Meter	Unit of Beat	First Division of Beat	Accents
2 4			
3 4			
4 4			
2 8			
3 8			
4 8			
2 2			
3 2			
4 2			

2. Write the correct note values where applicable in the various columns.

Meter	Four Beats	Three Beats	Two Beats	One Beat	Half a Beat	Three Thirds of a Beat	Quarter of a Beat	Eighth of a Beat
2/4								
3/4								
4/4 C								
2/2 ¢								
3/2								
4/2								
2/8								
3/8								
4/8								

50

3. a. Indicate the beat numbers and primary accents in a slow meter.

slow $\frac{6}{8}$ meter   ♪ ♪ ♪   ♪ ♪ ♪

b. Indicate the beat numbers and primary accents in a fast meter.

fast $\frac{6}{8}$ meter   ♪ ♪ ♪   ♪ ♪ ♪

c. In a slow $\frac{6}{8}$ meter which note receives one beat? _____

d. In a fast $\frac{6}{8}$ meter which note receives one beat? _____

e. In a slow $\frac{6}{4}$ meter which note receives one beat? _____

f. In a fast $\frac{6}{4}$ meter which note receives one beat? _____

g. Indicate the beat numbers and primary accents in a slow meter.

slow $\frac{6}{4}$ meter   ♩ ♩ ♩   ♩ ♩ ♩

h. Indicate the beat numbers and primary accents in a fast meter.

fast $\frac{6}{4}$ meter   ♩ ♩ ♩   ♩ ♩ ♩

i. In a fast $\frac{6}{8}$ meter what is the first division of the beat (♩.)?

j. In a fast $\frac{6}{4}$ meter what is the first division of the beat (♩.)?

4. Show the division and subdivision of undotted notes (simple meters).

Beat	Division of Beat	Subdivision of Beat
♩		
𝅗𝅥		
♪		

5. Show the division and subdivision of dotted notes (compound meters).

Beat	Division of Beat	Subdivision of Beat
𝅗𝅥.		
♩.		
♪.		

6. Where applicable, write the correct note or tied combination of notes for the number of beats indicated in slow compound meters.

7. Write the correct note or tied combination of notes for the number of beats indicated in fast compound meters.

6.

Meter	Twelve Beats	Nine Beats	Six Beats	Five Beats	Three Beats	Two Beats	One Beat	One Half Beat
6/8								
9/8								
12/8								
6/4								
9/4								
12/4								

7.

Meter	Four Beats	Three Beats	Two Beats	One Beat	Third of a Beat (First Division)
$\frac{6}{8}$					
$\frac{9}{8}$					
$\frac{12}{8}$					
$\frac{6}{4}$					
$\frac{9}{4}$					
$\frac{12}{4}$					

chapter

4

DEVELOPING
RHYTHMIC
RESPONSES

A practical ability in reading rhythmic notation may be achieved through the development of a rhythmic vocabulary and a definite feeling for the pulse or beat. The development of a rhythmic vocabulary is similar to the development of a word vocabulary. We recognize the printed word and know how to pronounce it. In music, we recognize a note in a given meter and learn to produce it for the correct duration. The acquisition of a rhythmic vocabulary will lead to the development of a vocabulary of rhythmic combinations or patterns which are referred to as the melodic rhythm.

The first step in achieving a rhythmic vocabulary which can be performed in a consistent manner lies in a strong and regular feeling for the beat. There are many ways in which this skill could be achieved but the one presented here is so basic that it should prove sufficient for all individuals.

Imagine that you are bouncing a ball on the floor. The motion employed is "down" (↓), "up" (↑). Say the words "down," "up" while using your arm. This technique will help to establish a feeling for a definite and steady beat. The complete "down" (↓), "up" (↑) motion will be equal to one full beat. The "down" (↓) motion will be equal to one half beat while the "up" (⬆) motion will also equal one half beat. If the meter signatures of $\frac{2}{4}$, $\frac{3}{4}$, $\frac{4}{4}$ or **C** are present, the quarter note will be the unit of beat. The quarter note will be held through the "down" (⬇), "up" (⬆) motion of the arm. If the pitch of A above Middle C is sounded and the musical syllable "do" is sung on each beat, a definite ability to sing quarter notes correctly will be accomplished. The pitch of A will be useful in learning rhythms since it is only one pitch and is generally around the middle of voice ranges.

Pitch of A above Middle C

The exercises which follow should use the "down", "up" motion of the arm and the syllable "do" sung at the pitch of A. "Do" is to be held through the complete "down," "up" motion of the arm. The order in which the exercises are taken is left to the discretion of the instructor. If preferred, the beat and its multiples may be studied before the divisions and subdivisions.

UNIT OF BEAT (♩ = 1 beat)

Sing this series of quarter-note rhythms using "do" as a neutral syllable combined with the "down" (⬇), "up" (⬆) motion of the arm.

Meter $\frac{4}{4}$

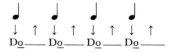

Note that singing with the "down" (⬇), "up" (⬆) motion of the arm mainly involves the vowel sound "o" part of "do," which is held until the top part of the (⬆) arrow is reached. Keep in mind that singing is largely concerned with tones that are produced on the vowel sounds: A (ah), E (eh), I (ee), O (oh), U (oo).

DIVISIONS AND SUBDIVISIONS OF THE BEAT

Division of the Beat (♩ = 1 beat)

Eighth notes—  —two equal tones to each beat. One "do" on "down" motion and one "do" on "up" motion.

Meter $\frac{4}{4}$

Do Do Do Do Do Do Do Do

Subdivision of the Beat (♩ = 1 beat)

Sixteenth notes—  —four equal tones to each beat. Two tones on "down" motion and two tones on "up" motion.

Meter $\frac{2}{4}$

Do Do Do Do Do Do Do Do

The technique of using words with an equivalent number of syllables will also prove helpful in gaining control of sixteenth notes. The word "al-li-ga-tor" has four syllables. Sing the word "al-li-ga-tor" on the pitch of A using the "down," "up" motion. Notice that this word has four syllables equivalent to the four sixteenth notes. Two syllables are sung on the "down" motion and two syllables are sung on the "up" motion.

Meter $\frac{2}{4}$

Al - li - ga - tor Al - li - ga - tor

Sing on the same pitch using "do-do-do-do" instead of the word "al-li-ga-tor." Notice that two "do's" are sung on the "down" motion and two "do's" are sung on the "up" motion.

Meter $\frac{2}{4}$

Do Do Do Do Do Do Do Do

A combination of quarter, eighth, and sixteenth notes will provide excellent practice material. Remember to include the "down," "up" motion of the arm for all rhythmic practice.

Meter $\frac{4}{4}$

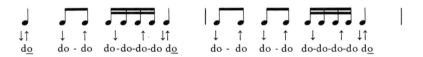

do   do - do   do-do-do-do do   do - do   do - do   do-do-do-do do

Other combinations of sixteenth-note rhythms may be secured through the "down," "up" motion of the arm and through a combination of unequal syllables in a word.

The combination of two sixteenth notes and one eighth note represents another division of the beat.

Meter $\frac{2}{4}$

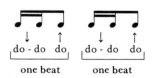

do - do do   do - do do

one beat   one beat

The word "ca-li-co" or the words "jing-le bells" in conjunction with the "down," "up" motion of the arm will help to establish this particular rhythmic combination.

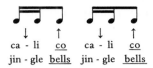

Another combination of the sixteenth-note and the eighth-note rhythms may be approached in a similar manner.

Meter $\frac{2}{4}$

The word "bot-a-ny" provides another example of using syllables in words to gain skill with this rhythmical combination.

Meter $\frac{2}{4}$

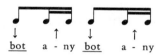

The following combination is more complex since the two sixteenth notes are not paired.

Meter $\frac{2}{4}$

In this combination the sixteenth note has the first half of the downbeat. The eighth note has the rest of the downbeat and half of the upbeat. The final sixteenth has the rest of the upbeat. Try dividing the downbeat into two equal halves and the upbeat also into two equal halves. Two down motions and two up motions of the arm are necessary. Do this exercise in slow motion before gradually increasing the speed.

Eventually, drop the subdivisions of the "down," "up" beats and perform this rhythmic pattern to single down and up arm motions as shown by the large arrows.

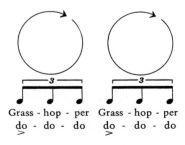

Leaving out one syllable in the word "alligator" may help in mastering this rhythm.

al - li - (ga) - tor

Other Divisions of the Beat

Triplet— ♪♪♪ —three equal tones to one beat.

A circular motion may be easier for the student in acquiring a feeling for the triplet in the beginning. Later the "down," "up" motion should be substituted. The difficulty with the "down," "up" is due to three notes equal to one third of a beat each fitting into the two equal halves of the "down," "up" motion. The clockwise beat makes it relatively simple. Using the circular motion and chanting or singing a three-syllable word will help to develop a response to the triplet.

Grass - hop - per   Grass - hop - per
do - do - do   do - do - do

After using the circular motion for the three equal tones to one beat, the student may then try to adapt each triplet to the "down," "up" motion which governs all rhythms. A first step in adapting the triplet to the "down," "up" beat so that a consistent pattern of beating time may be developed will be found by continuing to chant words of three syllables. Sing the word "grasshopper" on the pitch of A while using the "down," "up" motion of the arm. Now sing on the same pitch using "do-do-do" instead of "grasshopper" while using the arm motion. Accent the first note in each triplet. This is one way to achieve control of the triplet.

Relating to syllables in a word should help to develop a feeling for two variations of the triplet. The first example shows an eighth note (short) followed by a quarter note (long). Use the circular motion and sing on the pitch of A the two syllables in the word "duty." Sing the first syllable quickly and briefly hold the second syllable.

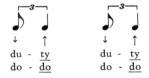

Note the difference in size of the arrows to emphasize the longer duration of the quarter note.

The second variant of the triplet shows a quarter note (long) followed by an eighth note (short). The first syllable in "maybe" is prolonged to achieve this rhythm.

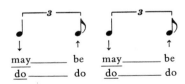

As before, drop the word association when feasible and use "do." Practice until the triplet variations can be executed with the "down," "up" motion as well as with the circular motion.

Multiples of the beat provide notes of longer duration.

Multiples of the Beat (♩ = 1 beat)

Half note— ♩ —one tone for two beats.

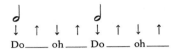

Do____ oh ____ Do ____ oh____

Dotted half note— ♩. —one tone for three beats.

Do____oh ____ oh ____ Do ____ oh ____ oh ____

Whole note— o —one tone for four beats.

Do____ oh ____ oh ____ oh ____ Do ____ oh ____ oh ____ oh ____

Unequal Rhythms

Dotted quarter note and eighth note— ♩. ♪ —two unequal tones to two beats.

Sing on the pitch of A. Push the "oh" slightly to emphasize the down (♦) portion of the second and fourth beats.

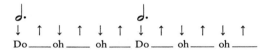

do-oh   do do-oh   do

Dotted eighth note and sixteenth note— ♪. ♪ —two unequal tones to one beat.

The dotted eighth note receives most of the beat while the sixteenth note receives the last portion of the up motion. Note the use of a small

extra arrow to indicate a separate quick note at the top of the up portion of the beat. An extra flick of the hand at the top of the beat may
accompany the extra arrow.

$$\frac{1}{4} + \frac{1}{4} + \frac{1}{4} + \frac{1}{4} = 1 \qquad \frac{3}{4} + \frac{1}{4} = 1$$

The ratio of the dotted eighth note to the sixteenth note is 3:1.

$$3 \ : \ 1 \qquad 3 \ : \ 1$$

Saying "an" on the last portion of the beats helps to shorten the
sixteenth note to the correct duration for a quarter of a beat. Try this
rhythm very slowly at first.

Meter $\frac{2}{4}$

one ____ an two ____ an

Note the small extra arrow for "an" to show the top portion of the
upbeat. It may be helpful to think of the sixteenth note as kicking
the next note a fraction before the new down motion begins. This results
in a type of skipping rhythm.

NEW UNIT OF BEAT ($\d$ = 1 beat)

The execution of the preceding rhythmic patterns was based on the
quarter note as the unit of beat. The same techniques, however, may be
employed to develop responses to comparable patterns when the unit of
beat is represented by another note. It is only necessary to determine
what kind of note represents the steady beat, and to recognize multiples,
divisions and subdivisions of it.

If, for example, the half note is the unit of beat, then two quarter notes become the equal division, four eighth notes become the equal subdivision, and the whole note is the steady beat doubled. The following illustrations should help to clarify the application of the techniques.

Half note— ♩ —one tone to one beat.

Meter ²⁄₂ (¢)

♩   ♩
↓ ↑ ↓ ↑
Do―― Do――

Division of the Beat (♩ = 1 beat)

Quarter notes— ♩ ♩ —two equal tones to one beat.
           ↓ ↑

Meter ²⁄₂ (¢)

♩ ♩ ♩ ♩
↓ ↑ ↓ ↑
Do- Do Do-Do

Subdivision of the Beat (♩ = 1 beat)

Eighth notes— —four equal tones to one beat.
           ↓   ↑

Meter ²⁄₂ (¢)

Do - Do - Do - Do   Do - Do- Do - Do
al - li - ga - tor   al - li - ga - tor

Variations of four equal tones to one beat:

Two eighth notes and quarter note— ♫ ♩
                              ↓   ↑

Meter $\frac{2}{2}$ (¢)

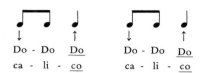

Do - Do Do   Do - Do Do
ca - li - co   ca - li - co

Quarter note and two eighth notes—

Meter $\frac{2}{2}$ (¢)

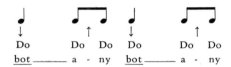

Do   Do Do Do   Do Do
bot ——— a - ny bot ——— a - ny

Eighth note, quarter note, and eighth note—

Meter $\frac{2}{2}$ (¢)

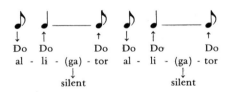

Do Do   Do Do Do   Do
al - li - (ga) - tor al - li - (ga) - tor
     silent   silent

Other Divisions of the Beat

Triplet— —three equal tones to one beat.

Meter $\frac{2}{2}$ (¢)

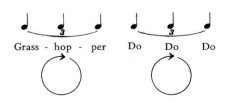

Grass - hop - per   Do   Do   Do

Variations of the triplet:

Quarter note and half note— 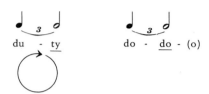 —two unequal tones to one beat.

Meter $\frac{2}{2}$ (¢)

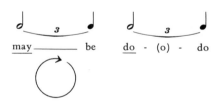

du - ty   do - do - (o)

Half note and quarter note— 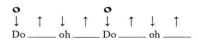 —two unequal tones to one beat.

Meter $\frac{2}{2}$ (¢)

may _____ be   do - (o) - do

Multiples of the Beat (♩ = 1 beat)

Whole note— o —one tone to two beats.

Meter $\frac{4}{2}$

Do _____ oh _____ Do _____ oh _____

Dotted whole note— **o·** —one tone to three beats.

Meter $\frac{6}{2}$

o·   **o·**
↓   ↑   ↓   ↑   ↓   ↑   ↓   ↑   ↓   ↑   ↓   ↑
Do_____ o _____ o _____ Do _____ o _____ o _____

Unequal Rhythms

Dotted half note and quarter note— ♩· ♩ —two unequal tones to two beats.

Meter $\frac{4}{2}$

♩·   ♩ ♩·   ♩
↓   ↑   ↓   ↑   ↓   ↑   ↓   ↑
Do_____ oh Do Do_____ oh Do

Dotted quarter note and eighth note— ♩· ♪ —two unequal tones to one beat.

Meter $\frac{2}{2}$

♩·   ♪ ♩·   ♪
↓   ↑   ↑   ↓   ↑   ↑
Do   Do Do   Do
(One   an two   an)

Note the small extra arrows to show the top portion of the upbeat.

The following table compares similar rhythms when the unit of beat changes. These are some of the more common rhythmic patterns.

Table X: Comparable Rhythms

A. Unit of Beat and Its Multiples

Unit of Beat	One Tone to Two Beats	One Tone to Three Beats	One Tone to Four Beats	One Tone to Six Beats
𝅘𝅥	𝅗𝅥	𝅗𝅥.	𝅝	
𝅗𝅥	𝅝	𝅝.	𝅜	
𝅘𝅥𝅮	𝅘𝅥	𝅘𝅥.	𝅗𝅥	𝅗𝅥.
𝅘𝅥.	𝅗𝅥.		𝅝.	
𝅗𝅥.	𝅝.			

B. Unit of Beat and its Equal Divisions and Subdivisions

Meter	Unit of Beat	Two Equal Tones to One Beat	Three Equal Tones to One Beat	Four Equal Tones to One Beat
2/4	♩	♫	♪♪♪ (3)	♬
2/2	𝅗𝅥	♩ ♩	♩♩♩ (3)	♫
3/8	♪	♬	♪♪♪ (3)	♬
6/8 (slow)	♪.	♪♪ (2)	♪♪♪	
6/8 (fast)	♪.	♩ ♩ (2)	♪ ♪ ♪	
6/4	𝅗𝅥.			

69

C. Unit of Beat and Its Unequal Divisions and Subdivisions

Meter	Unit of Beat	Two Unequal Tones to One Beat	Three Unequal Tones to One Beat
$\frac{2}{4}$	♩	♪. 𝅘𝅥𝅯	𝅘𝅥𝅯𝅘𝅥𝅯♪, ♪𝅘𝅥𝅯𝅘𝅥𝅯, 𝅘𝅥𝅯♪𝅘𝅥𝅯
$\frac{2}{2}$	𝅗𝅥	♩. ♪	♪♪♩, ♩♪♪, ♪♩♪
$\frac{3}{8}$ $\frac{6}{8}$ (slow)	♪	𝅘𝅥𝅯. 𝅘𝅥𝅰	𝅘𝅥𝅰𝅘𝅥𝅰𝅘𝅥𝅯, 𝅘𝅥𝅯𝅘𝅥𝅰𝅘𝅥𝅰, 𝅘𝅥𝅰𝅘𝅥𝅯𝅘𝅥𝅰
$\frac{3}{8}$ $\frac{6}{8}$ (fast)	♩.	♩ ♪ or ♪ ♩	
$\frac{6}{4}$ (fast)	𝅗𝅥.	𝅗𝅥 ♩ or ♩ 𝅗𝅥	

D. Two Unequal Tones to Two Beats

Meter	Unit of Beat	Two Unequal Tones to Two Beats	
2 / 4	♩	1 2 and	
2 / 2	𝅗𝅥	1 2 and	
3 / 8 6 / 8 (slow)	♪	1 2 and	

DUPLET AND TRIPLET SIGNS

The duplet indications are needed to divide a dotted note into two equal parts. The normal division of the dotted note is into three equal notes. The duplet, when the dotted note is the unit of beat, is an irregular division of the beat and is found in a compound meter.

Meter	Unit of Beat	First Division	Unit of Beat	Duplet (Irregular Division)	Duplet Sign
6 8	♩.	♪♪♪	♩.	♫ 2	2

The triplet indications are needed when the undotted note is the unit of beat, since the normal division is into two equal parts. The triplet will be found most often in a simple meter signature, where the undotted note will be the unit of beat.

Meter	Unit of Beat	First Division	Unit of Beat	Triplet (Subdivision)
2 4	♩	♪♪	♩	♪♪♪ 3
2 2	♩	♩ ♩	♩	♩♩♩ 3

The "down," "up" motion of the arm involves one other consideration. The down motion is always the beat whether it is the first, second, third, or fourth beat of the measure. If the downbeat occurs on the first beat of a measure, we say "one." If the downbeat occurs on the second beat of the measure, we say "two." In other words, all downbeats represent a specific beat number within each measure. All that is necessary is to determine on which beat of a measure the downbeat occurs.

The upbeat can be stated as "and."

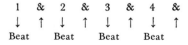

```
1    &    2    &    3    &    4    &
↓    ↑    ↓    ↑    ↓    ↑    ↓    ↑
Beat      Beat      Beat      Beat
```

With this technique, it is possible to combine the arm motion with specific beat numbers in each measure as well as the upbeats, which are now recognized as the second half of each beat.

Sing these exercises on the pitch of A, using the beat numbers for downbeats with "and" for all upbeats.

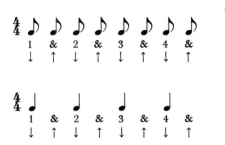

Remember to give each quarter note a full beat of "down," "up."

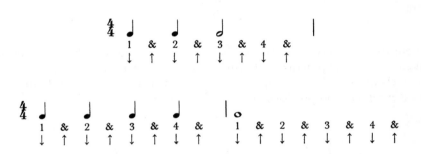

Eventually, it will be possible for the student to drop the "and," but it is of value in the beginning in sensing the duration value of each rhythm.

SYNCOPATION

Syncopation results when the accent (>) occurs on the up (↑) part of the beat rather than the down (↓). In a normal placement of accents in a pattern of eighth notes, they would occur on the down part of each beat as indicated by arrows.

Normally, quarter notes would have accents on the first beat of each measure with some stress on the down part of each beat.

A combination of eighth and quarter notes will demonstrate the displaced accent called syncopation.

Note that the accent occurs on the "and" (&) of the first beat. A simple sketch and some practice will result in a grasp of syncopation.

Using the "down," "up" arm motion for each beat, try chanting the beat numbers and portions of the beat on the pitch of A.

Sing:

Try the syncopation in ⅔ meter using the same process. Pitch of A:

MORE ON DOTS, TIES, AND BEAMS

A dot may not be used if it extends the value of a note over the bar line and into the next measure. In such a case, the tie should be used.

When joining flagged notes, it is advisable to beam them in units of single beats. This practice will provide greater clarity in reading the division into halves, thirds, and quarters of each beat.

INCOMPLETE MEASURES

Incomplete measures generally indicate that a section of the music will begin with an upbeat. This is referred to in music as the anacrusis. In this case, the rhythmic value needed for the upbeat is borrowed from the last measure in the section. An example of this is in "America the Beautiful," which has one quarter note as an upbeat at the beginning of the song. The value of this note is only one beat. Obviously, this is an incomplete measure.

AMERICA THE BEAUTIFUL

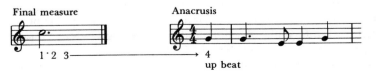

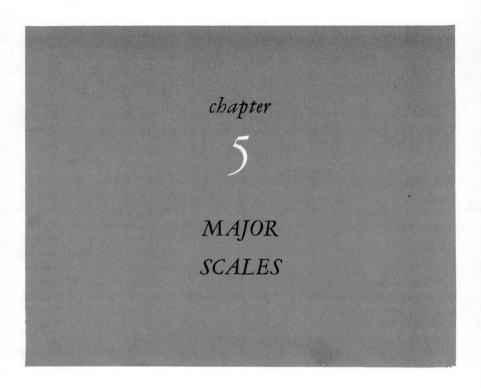

All musical composition has been governed by certain established formulas or patterns from the melody types of ancient Greece: the Greek modes, the Pythagorean scale devised by the Greek mathematician Pythagoras (about 550 B.C.), the medieval church modes of the Catholic Church, and finally the scales found in the great body of music in Western culture. Volumes could be written on the evolutionary phases of the organized patterns in music. We will limit ourselves to a detailed account of the arrangement of tones currently in use which are called scales. There are several types of scales involved in our music: major scales, minor scales, chromatic scale, whole tone scale, and pentatonic scale. Some of the more advanced music of the twentieth century has produced new patterns in place of the traditional scales, but the scales as we know them still account for a major share of new music.

The musical scale is correctly named, for the word "scale" actually means ladder. In music, a scale is an ascending or a descending arrangement of notes which have been mathematically derived. All major scales have the same formula of whole and half steps. By whole step we mean the distance on the piano keyboard from one white key to the next white key with a black key between.

Example:

If there is no black key in between, the distance is only a half step, as is the case with **E** to **F** and **B** to **C**. Other half steps occur between a

white key and a neighboring black key 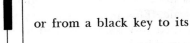 or from a black key to its neighboring white key.

One white key to the next white key with a black key between them is a whole step. Two black keys with a single white key between them is also a whole step.

The whole and half steps found in the scale are portrayed on our musical ladder, which is a parallel to the staff.

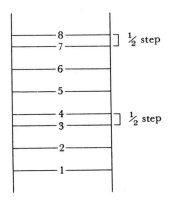

The major scale as shown on the ladder has eight notes. Attention is directed to the 3rd and 4th, 7th and 8th rungs of the ladder. The distance between 3 and 4 is one half step and the same is true between

7 and 8. All others are whole steps. We may deduce from this that all major scales have half steps between 3 and 4 and 7 and 8, with whole steps between 1 and 2, 2 and 3, 4 and 5, 5 and 6, 6 and 7. Simply stated, half steps between 3 and 4, 7 and 8; all others whole steps.

We will use the Latin syllables traditionally found in singing—do, re, mi, fa, sol, la, ti, do—and the corresponding Arabic numerals—1, 2, 3, 4, 5, 6, 7, 8—which will be of value in the determination of the whole and half steps. (Note that "do"—the first note of the scale—is repeated at the top to complete the scale.)

In every major scale there is one principal tone upon which the scale is built and which identifies the pitch name or key name of the scale. This principal or key tone is the first degree of the scale and is called "do." Since we will be using Latin syllables and Arabic numerals, it will be necessary to see them on the musical ladder.

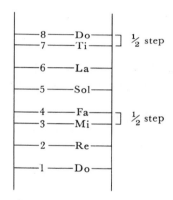

"C" MAJOR SCALE

The following procedure will be followed in constructing all of the major scales.

1. Locate Middle C on the piano keyboard. (Middle C is the key-note here but other scales will involve different keynotes).

2. Write Middle C on the treble staff and low C eight tones lower on the bass staff.

3. On consecutive lines and spaces, draw eight whole notes beginning on C on both treble and bass staves.

4. Under each note, write the appropriate letter name.

5. Place a bracket over 3–4 and 7–8 on the treble staff. Inside the brackets, write ⌐½ step⌐ .

6. Place a bracket under 3–4 and 7–8 on the bass staff. Inside the brackets, write ⌐½ step⌐ .

On the piano keyboard you will find the distance between the notes of the "C" Major scale to be:

    1 and 2 (C–D) is two half steps   (whole step)
    2 and 3 (D–E) is two half steps   (whole step)
    3 and 4 (E–F) is one half step
    4 and 5 (F–G) is two half steps   (whole step)
    5 and 6 (G–A) is two half steps   (whole step)
    6 and 7 (A–B) is two half steps   (whole step)
    7 and 8 (B–C) is one half step

The complete step formula for the construction of any major scale is:

$$\text{step—step—half step—step—step—step—half step}$$

Expressed in numerals the step formula is:

$$1\text{--}1\text{--}\tfrac{1}{2}\text{--}1\text{--}1\text{--}1\text{--}\tfrac{1}{2}$$

Since we are going to build all major scales from this formula, it will be necessary to use the piano keyboard provided with this text as a visual guide in building these scales. The musical ladder and the formula showing the size of the steps in the major scale will also assist the student in the construction of major scales.

LEADING TONE

Attention is directed toward the keynote or "do." It is a point of magnetic attraction since it establishes the pitch level or key. It is also called the tonic. The strong pull of the keynote is best demonstrated by playing the notes of the "C" Major scale up to the seventh tone ("ti") and lingering on this tone before going to the top note of the scale ("do"). Notice the finality of the sound once the upper "do" is reached. The seventh tone of the scale ("ti") is one half step away from "do" and is strongly attracted to "do." The seventh tone of the major scale must be raised by a chromatic if it is more than one half step away from "do." The seventh tone is called the leading tone in major scales. The presence of a leading tone ensures finality once the keynote is reached. The absence of a leading tone gives an elusive effect that is more typical of other types of scales which will appear later.

Before any attempt is made to construct all the major scales it will be necessary to discuss some of the signs involved in the process.

CHROMATIC SIGNS

There are five basic signs found in music notation which indicate the whole and half steps found in major scales. They are:

The sharp ♯, which raises the pitch of a tone one half step.

The flat ♭, which lowers the pitch of a tone one half step.

The natural ♮ (also called a cancel), which removes the effect of a previous sharp or flat. When the ♮ removes a ♯ the pitch is lowered one half step; when the ♮ removes a ♭ the pitch is raised one half step.

The double sharp, which may be written ♯♯ or ✗. The double sharp raises the pitch of a tone two half steps (whole step). Sometimes we find that a note is already sharped in the key signature. When this occurs, one of the two sharps in the double sharp is considered to be a duplicate of the same sharp in the key signature. This is merely a reminder that the tone in question has previously been raised one half step.

The double flat ♭♭, which lowers the pitch of a tone two half steps (whole step). If a particular note has been flatted in the key signature, one of the two flats is considered to be a duplicate of the same flat in the key signature.

Attention is directed to the fact that a ♯, ♭, ♮, ♯♯ (✗), or ♭♭ affects every note on the same line or space in the same measure. When the bar line is reached, the chromatic sign is no longer in effect. The key signature, which will be presented in this chapter, then becomes the authority for the whole and half steps.

If any note is sharped or flatted in the key signature, all notes bearing the same letter name will be sharped or flatted. A sharp on the fifth line (F), for example, will mean that all Fs will be sharped whether they are on the same line, the first space, or even higher or lower.

All chromatic signs are placed on the left side of the notes involved and should be on the same line or space as the note.

The construction of major scales sometimes shows the keynote sharped on the bottom of the scale ("do") and again on the top of the scale (upper "do"). One of the two sharps (the lower) is considered to be a duplicate and is not counted when totaling the number of sharps in a given scale. The same is true with flats. If 1 (low "do") and 8 (upper "do") are both flatted, only one flat is counted in the total.

DOMINANT RELATIONSHIP

The construction of scales involving the use of sharps can be accomplished progressively by beginning each new scale on a pitch five letter names away from the previous letter name. Following this procedure, we count five consecutive letter names of the alphabet starting with C. We find that the next scale after "C" Major is "G" Major. All major scales involving sharps are determined in this manner. This orderly progression of scales involving sharps may be seen on the half circle which follows. Notice that the letter names for each new scale using sharps are going clockwise around the circle and are five letter names away from each other. Each previous letter name is counted as one in establishing the new letter name.

The word "dominant" in music refers to a pitch that is five letter names above (going clockwise), or five letter names below (going counterclockwise), the previous pitch. The letter names found by going clockwise around the circle are referred to as the upper dominants and involve the sharp (♯). Going counterclockwise and backwards in the alphabet will produce the subdominants or lower dominants, which involve the flat (♭). The lower dominants will be presented in the section on scales involving flats.

Upper Dominant Key Names

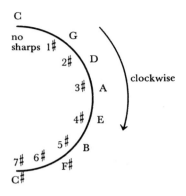

Note:

1. The distance between each letter name is five letter names, counting the previous letter name as one.
2. Counting the half steps between the letter names on the piano keyboard will show that the distance of a fifth between them is actually seven half steps.
3. Counting seven half steps from B produces F♯.
4. Counting seven half steps from F♯ produces C♯.

CONSTRUCTING MAJOR SCALES WITH SHARPS

The formula used in conjunction with the piano keyboard produced the "C" Major scale. The same formula applied to the piano keyboard will produce all of the major scales. There are fifteen major scales including "C" Major. Seven major scales involve the use of the sharp chromatic sign (♯) to create the whole and half steps of the formula. Seven major scales involve the use of the flat chromatic sign (♭) to create the whole and half steps of the formula. The key of "C" does not need sharps or flats, since the whole and half steps beginning with C follow the formula naturally. The half steps between E and F, B and C are already present on the piano keyboard and do not have to be altered. Counting up five letter names from C will produce the pitch name G, which is the keynote for the scale of "G." The scale formula will establish the need for one sharp to create a half step between 7–8.

"G" Major Scale

Constructing a major scale on the pitch of G, which is five letter names or seven half steps above "C" Major going clockwise on the cycle, will demonstrate the practicality of the formula when used with the piano keyboard.

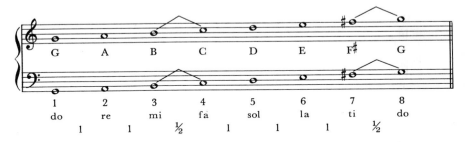

Note:

1. G is the keynote.
2. The sharp is added to make a whole step between E and F♯ ("la"–"ti"), 6–7, as called for in the scale formula.
3. F♯ (seventh tone) is the leading tone, one half step away from the keynote G ("do" or 8).
4. Half steps between B and C ("mi"–"fa"), 3–4; and between F♯ and G ("ti"–"do"), 7–8.
5. The keynote names the key. The key of one sharp is the key of "G" Major.

"D" Major

Our next key will involve the use of two sharps.

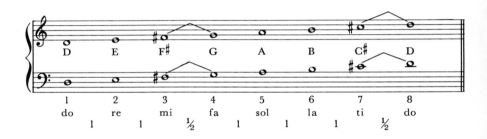

Note:

1. D is the keynote.
2. Two sharps are added to conform to the scale formula: F♯ to create a a half step between F♯ and G ("mi"–"fa"), 3–4.
3. C♯ to create a half step between C♯ and D ("ti"–"do"), 7–8.
4. Whole steps between E and F♯ ("re"–"mi"), 2–3; and between B and C♯ ("la"–"ti"), 6–7.
5. C♯ is the leading tone.
6. The keynote names the key. The key of two sharps is D.

We shall learn how to assemble key signatures shortly, but for the present, the value of this approach lies in the increasing knowledge of how scales are built. Key signatures are derived from this knowledge of scale structure.

The student should now build all the major scales using the sharp chromatic to produce the whole and half steps found in the major scale formula. The pitch name for each of these major scales using sharps will be found in the exercises at the end of this chapter. These exercises should be completed before the scales using flats in their structure are encountered. Remember that the keynote F♯ (low "do") will be duplicated at the top of the scale also as F♯ (upper "do"). Only one of the two sharps (the upper) is counted in the total. A further discussion of this duplication will develop in the later section on key signatures. The same duplication occurs in the scale constructed on C♯.

CONSTRUCTING MAJOR SCALES USING FLATS

The formula used as a guide in constructing the major scales with sharps will also serve as a guide in the construction of the seven major scales which involve the flat chromatic.

The first step will be to establish the keynote for each successive major scale using flats. The letter names are still determined by the distance of five letter names away from the name of the keynote in the previous major scale using flats. However, there is a distinct difference in the process at this point. Each new letter name is found by going backwards in the alphabet and counting down seven half steps from the previous keynote. Going counterclockwise on the circle and backwards in the alphabet produces the descending pattern which leads to the next keynote. These are called the subdominant or lower dominant keys.

Subdominant Key Names (Lower Dominants)

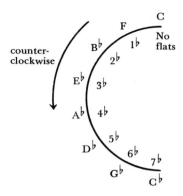

The descending pattern of seven half steps from the previous key-note C determines the keynote F. Applying the formula for major scales to the keynote F will establish the major scale of "F," which has one flat. This scale utilizes one flat to make the half step between 3 and 4. The half step between 7 and 8 is already present and does not need alteration, since E to F on the piano keyboard is a half step.

"F" Major

F	G	A	B♭	C	D	E	F
1	2	3	4	5	6	7	8
do	re	mi	fa	sol	la	ti	do

1   1   ½   1   1   1   ½

Note:

1. The keynote is F.
2. The flat is added to B to create the half step between A and B♭ (3–4 or "mi"–"fa").
3. E (seventh tone) is the leading tone, one half step away from the key-note F ("do" or 8).
4. No chromatic was needed between 7 and 8, since E and F are already one half step apart on the piano keyboard.
5. The keynote names the key. The key of one flat is the key of "F" Major.

One further example is necessary before the construction of all major scales using flats is undertaken. We have found that counting down seven half steps from C and going backwards in the alphabet resulted in the keynote F. When you count down seven half steps from F going backwards in the alphabet, something additional is involved. Not only is the letter name B produced, but we must place a flat next to its name, since seven half steps below F is actually the black key B♭ on the piano keyboard. Completing the counterclockwise succession of major keys using flats will show that the keys involving two through seven flats will have a flat added to each new key name seven half steps below the previous key name. The only flat key that does not have a flat added to the key name is the key of one flat, "F" Major.

The student is advised to verify this by counting down seven half steps from each previous key using the piano keyboard. The result in each case should be the same as the key names provided in the subdominant portion of the circle.

The scale of "B♭" Major will provide a further example before other major scales using flats are constructed.

"B♭" Major

The key of two flats.

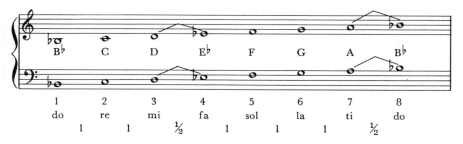

Note:

1. The keynote is B♭.
2. The flat is added to E to create the half step between D and E♭ ("mi"–"fa"), 3–4.
3. The flat is added to B to create the half step between A and B♭ ("ti"–"do"), 7–8.
4. The leading tone is A.
5. The keynote names the key. The key of two flats is the key of B♭.
6. When a flat is duplicated, only one flat—the upper one—is counted in the total.
7. All flat keys which follow will have a flat added to the letter name.

The student should now proceed to the exercises at the end of this chapter which require the use of flats in the construction of the major scales. These exercises should be completed before progressing to the next section on the construction of key signatures.

PLACEMENT OF SHARPS IN KEY SIGNATURES

Our next consideration will be the placement of sharps for key signatures on the treble staff. Once the skill of building major scales has been accomplished, it is relatively easy to extract the sharps and arrange them in a pattern which becomes a key signature. Sharps in a key signature are placed in a zigzag pattern ♯♯♯ and are not directly over or under other sharps. There is a simple formula for placing sharps on the treble staff. The first sharp always goes on the fifth line (F). The formula for adding sharps is *down four, up five,* except the key of five sharps, which shows the last sharp going down four rather than up five.

First ♯ goes on fifth line.
Second ♯ goes on third space (down four).
Third ♯ goes on fifth space or space above staff (up five).
Fourth ♯ goes on fourth line (down four).
Fifth ♯ goes on second space (down four)—exception.
Sixth ♯ goes on fourth space (up five).
Seventh ♯ goes on third line (down four).

The formula proceeds for the most part on the basis of *down four, up five* with the exception of the key of five sharps, which breaks the rule to avoid placing the fifth sharp too high above the staff.

Here, the last sharp is A in both cases, but we went down four to avoid going off the staff. Remember that in the writing of the key signature of four sharps and five sharps, both go down four. Always count the previous sharp as one. The magic number in music is nine. If five is subtracted from nine, the result is four. This will be discussed later when intervals are presented. Suffice it to say that the net result is that we produce the same note whether we go up five or down four. The difference is that they are an octave apart.

The students' attention is drawn to the fact that building scales sometimes calls for low "do" and high "do" to have a sharp. If both low "do" and high "do" require a sharp, we consider one of these sharps to be a repetition. In that case, we place the sharp for the upper "do" in the key signature.

The sharps in the key signature tell us to sharp every note having the same letter name whether it is on a line or a space.

Example: If low "do" is F♯ (first space),

high "do" will also be F♯ (fifth line)

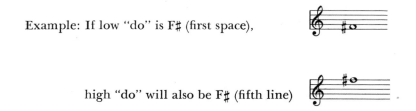

Both "do's" are named F♯ but only the upper F♯ is shown in the key signature. This F♯ is all we need to show that all notes on the F line or space are also F♯s.

The preceding table proceeds for the most part on the basis of *down four, up five* with the exception of the key of B, which breaks the rule to avoid placing the fifth sharp too high above the staff.

Sharp Key Signatures on the Bass Staff

Once the first sharp is placed on the fourth line (F) of the bass staff, the placement of sharps on the bass staff follows the same *down four, up five* pattern of the treble staff. The key of five sharps breaks the rule and goes down four. This will retain the pattern established in the treble staff, although counting up five would not force us to go off the staff.

First ♯ goes on fourth line.
Second ♯ goes on second space (down four).
Third ♯ goes on fourth space (up five).
Fourth ♯ goes on third line (down four).
Fifth ♯ goes on first space (down four)—exception.
Sixth ♯ goes on third space (up five).
Seventh ♯ goes on second line (down four).

PLACEMENT OF FLATS IN KEY SIGNATURES

Flat Key Signatures on the Treble Staff

The placement of flats on the treble staff also follows a pattern, but unlike the placement of sharps, there is no deviation from this formula. Once the first flat is placed on the third line (B), the pattern is *up four, down five* with no exception. Always count the previous flat as one.

First ♭ goes on third line.
Second ♭ goes on fourth space (up four).
Third ♭ goes on second space (down five).
Fourth ♭ goes on fourth line (up four).
Fifth ♭ goes on second line (down five).
Sixth ♭ goes on third space (up four).
Seventh ♭ goes on first space (down five).

The student's attention is now directed to the fact that in all flat keys except the key of one flat, both high and low "do" are flatted, but only the upper flat is placed in the key signature. Any note that is flatted in the key signature indicates that all notes having the same letter name will be flatted whether they are high or low, or whether they are on a line or a space. Notice that all the flats used in these key signatures on the treble staff are contained within the staff.

Flat Key Signatures on the Bass Staff

The first flat is always placed on the second line on the bass staff. Key of one flat:

The placement of all other flats follows the formula of *up four, down five*. Always count the previous flat as one.

First ♭ goes on second line.
Second ♭ goes on third space (up four).
Third ♭ goes on first space (down five).
Fourth ♭ goes on third line (up four).
Fifth ♭ goes on first line (down five).
Sixth ♭ goes on second space (up four).
Seventh ♭ goes on space below the staff (down five).

CYCLE OF MAJOR KEYS

The complete cycle of major keys is a valuable memory aid in learning key signatures. Reading clockwise, we find the sharp key signatures. Reading counterclockwise, we find the flat key signatures.

Starting with the key of "C," we go clockwise and count up five for each successive sharp key signature. Starting with the key of "C" going counterclockwise, we count down five for each successive flat key signature. In each instance, count the preceding key as number one.

Going clockwise, each successive key is called the dominant of the preceding key (distance up of seven half steps). Going counterclockwise, each successive key is called the subdominant of the preceding key (distance down of seven half steps).

The cycle of keys telescopes a large amount of the material presented on key signatures into a concise guide for the student. The only additional knowledge required is found in the section dealing with the placement of sharps and flats in the various key signatures, which can be reduced to the two formulas and the exceptions.

Cycle of Keys

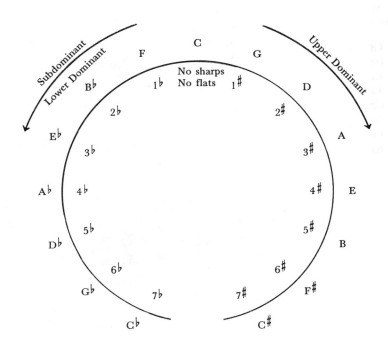

ENHARMONIC EQUIVALENTS

When two scales having different key signatures use the same keys on the piano, they are considered to be enharmonic equivalents. For instance, the major key of "C♯" is the enharmonic equivalent of "D♭" Major, since both keys use identical piano keys to produce their separate scales. This is also true for the major keys of "F♯" and "G♭," "C♭" and "B".

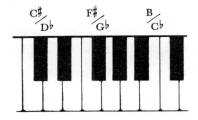

Individual notes may be considered the enharmonic equivalents of other notes:

C♯ = D♭
D♯ = E♭
E♯ = F
F♯ = G♭
G♯ = A♭
A♯ = B♭
C♭ = B
B♯ = C

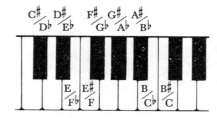

The specific choice of an enharmonic equivalent will be determined by the context of the music in which it is to be used.

FINDING "DO" AND THE KEY NAME

"Do" With Sharps

Another approach to learning the names of keys lies in the ability to find "do" in each key. There are two basic steps involved. The first step involves sharp key signatures. The last sharp, farthest to the right from the clef sign, is "ti" of the scale. To find "do," simply count up one. The letter name of the line or space upon which "do" is found *plus* any sharp that occurs on that line or space in the key signature will name the key.

Examples:

1. **Key of seven sharps:**

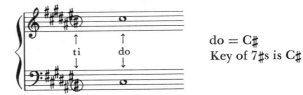

do = C♯
Key of 7♯s is C♯

2. **Key of six sharps:**

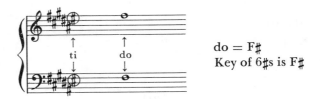

do = F♯
Key of 6♯s is F♯

3. **Key of five sharps:**

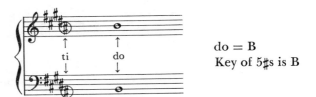

do = B
Key of 5♯s is B

4. **Key of four sharps:**

do = E
Key of 4♯s is E

5. Key of three sharps:

do = A
Key of 3♯s is A

Notice the position of "ti" in the key of three sharps, especially on the treble staff. When "ti" is rather high, we count down to low "do" rather than up since we do not want "do" to be above the staff at this time.

6. Key of two sharps:

do = D
Key of 2♯s is D

7. Key of one sharp:

do = G
Key of 1♯ is G

Notice the position of "ti." Since "ti" is rather high we count down to "do" to keep it on the staff.

"Do" With Flats

Finding "do" in flat key signatures will complete our work with major key names. To find "do" in the flat key signatures, we find the second to last flat or the flat second to last to the right of the clef sign. The letter name of the line or space upon which "do" is found *plus* any flat that occurs on that line or space in the signature will name the key.

Examples:

1. Key of seven flats:

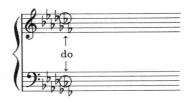

do = C♭
Key of 7♭s is C♭

2. Key of six flats:

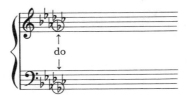

do = G♭
Key of 6♭s is G♭

3. Key of five flats:

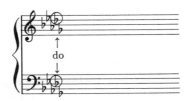

do = D♭
Key of 5♭s is D♭

4. Key of four flats:

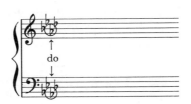

do = A♭
Key of 4♭s is A♭

5. Key of three flats:

do = E♭
Key of 3♭s is E♭

6. Key of two flats:

do = B♭
Key of 2♭s is B♭

7. Key of one flat:

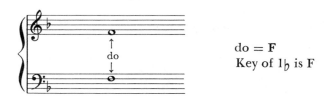

do = F
Key of 1♭ is F

The key signature of one flat obviously does not have a second to last flat. The student should memorize the name of the key of one flat as F.

There is another system of finding "do" with flats. Consider the last flat as "fa" of the scale and then count up or down to "do." The problem with this method is that it involves an additional step in counting. A single misstep in counting will result in an incorrect placement for "do."

This method may be of some help in remembering the keynote for the key of one flat, since the only flat in the signature is "fa."

Keynote

Exercises

1. Build major scales from the given notes and use sharp chromatics where necessary. Use the piano keyboard as a guide for the whole and half steps found in the major scale pattern. Do not use key signatures.

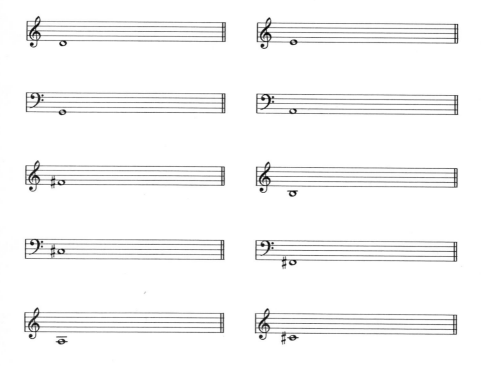

2. a. Arrange the sharp chromatics found in the previous scales as key signatures. Remember to place each sharp according to the rules for sharp key signatures.
   b. Place "do" and name each key.

3. Build major scales from the given notes and use flat chromatics where necessary. Do not use key signatures.

4. a. Arrange the flat chromatics found in the previous scales as key signatures. Remember to place each flat according to the rules for flat key signatures.

   b. Place "do" and name each key.

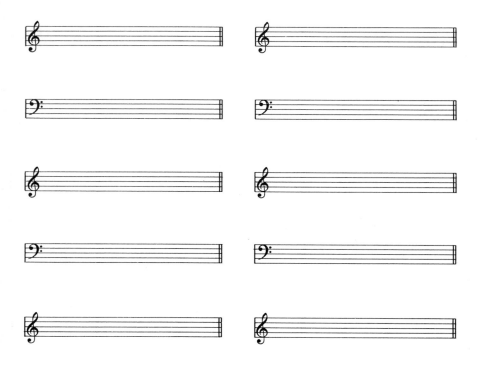

5. Construct the cycle of major keys. Place the key names on the outside of the circle and indicate the correct number of sharps or flats within the circle.

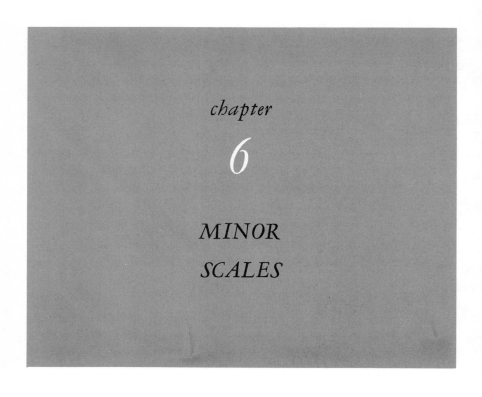

MINOR SCALES

chapter

6

RELATIVE MINOR KEYS

Natural Minor

Minor scales resemble major scales in that they also have seven basic tones with an added eighth tone—a duplication of the first note an octave higher. Minor scales also resemble major scales through the use of a key signature that is common to both. Every major keynote ("do") will have a relative minor keynote ("la"), which is found one and one half steps below the major keynote.

The piano keyboard will verify that the distance between the major keynote "C" ("do") and the minor keynote "a" ("la") is one and one half steps.

Keynotes will share a common key signature. The difference between the two lies in the emphasis placed on the individual keynotes. The major scale emphasizes "do" and encompasses the whole and half steps from low "do" to the upper "do" an octave higher. The example presented provides the formula for the whole and half steps of the major scale.

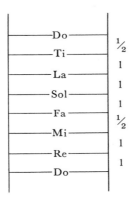

The minor scale emphasizes "la" and involves varying sizes in the steps from the lower "la" to the upper "la" an octave higher.

The musical ladder for the basic form of the minor scale provides a formula which indicates the close relationship between major and minor scales. This particular form of the minor scale is called the "natural minor." There are two other forms to be presented later which merely involve the chromatic alteration of some of the notes found in the basic natural minor scale.

Natural Minor Scale Formula:

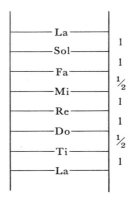

A comparison of the position of the whole and half steps of the major scale with those of the natural minor scale will show the same half steps between "ti" and "do," and between "mi" and "fa." However, "ti" is not used as a leading tone on the seventh note of the minor scale. "Ti" is now the second tone in minor rather than the seventh tone as it is in major. In other words, the natural minor scale does not have a leading tone, since "sol" is one whole step away from "la." This particular minor scale form creates an elusive antique sound which is due to the absence of a leading tone. Arabic numerals and Latin syllables indicate the various degrees in each scale.

"C" Major Scale

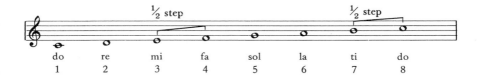

"a" Natural Minor

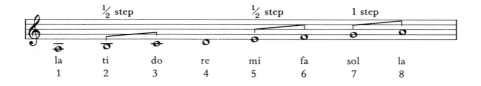

Note:

1. Both scales have the same key signature.
2. The distance between the respective keynotes is one and one half steps.
3. The scale tones in the natural minor are the same scale tones found in major except the range for minor is "la" to "la" rather than "do" to "do."
4. The half steps in both the major scale and the relative natural minor scale have the same letter names but they occur on different degrees in each form.
5. "Ti" does not function as a leading tone since there is no leading tone in the natural minor scale.
6. "Sol" (7) to "la" (8) is one whole step in the natural minor.

At this point, the exercises provided for all natural minor scales at the end of this chapter should be attempted. Remember that all natural minor scales will be based on a keynote one and one half steps below the major keynote. The key signature will provide the basic whole and half steps of the natural minor scale. All that is necessary is to find "la" in each key and write the scale tones in consecutive order with no alterations.

Harmonic Minor

The magnetic pull of "ti" (7) to "do" (8) in the major scale is paralleled in the second form of the minor scale, which is called the harmonic minor. Raising the seventh tone ("sol") of the natural minor scale one half step will create a leading tone for this scale which is one half step away from the keynote "la" (8). The original seventh tone ("sol") is now called "si," which is a Latin syllable indicating a tone one half step above "sol." If there is no sharp or flat on the letter name for "sol" in the key signature, we use a sharp (♯) chromatic to raise "sol" one half step. In the "a" harmonic minor example, a sharp is used to raise "sol" (G), since the "G" is not sharped in the key signature.

"a" Harmonic Minor

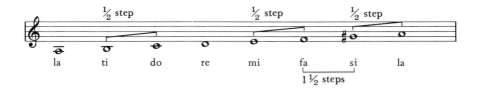

Note:

1. Basically, the form is the same as the natural minor except for the creation of a leading tone ("si") which is strongly pulling toward the keynote ("la").
2. There is a larger distance between "fa" and "si" (one and a half steps) than there is between "fa" and "sol" (one step).
3. The half steps ("mi–fa" and "ti–do") are the same for harmonic minor and natural minor.

Harmonic Minor Scale Formula:

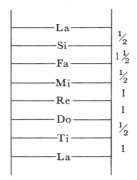

The construction of the harmonic minor scale is basically the same as the construction of the natural minor scale. The only change occurs on the seventh tone of the minor scale. "Sol" must be raised one half step to create a leading tone. However, some attention must be directed toward the selection of the proper chromatic sign necessary to create a tone one half step above "sol." The following guide is provided for that purpose:

1. If the letter name for "sol" in a given key does not have a sharp or a flat in the key signature (which was placed there to make it "sol" in the first place), the sharp (♯) is used to create "si," one half step above "sol."

2. If the letter name for "sol" has a sharp (♯) attached to it in the key signature (which provides the proper distance for "sol"), the double sharp is used to raise "sol" one half step. The double sharp is written ♯♯ or 𝄪.

3. If the letter name for "sol" has a flat (♭) in the key signature (which was provided to make the proper distance for "sol"), then the cancel or natural (♮) sign is used to remove the effect of the flat in the key signature. Removing the effect of the flat raises the pitch one half step. This produces the leading tone "si." The example which follows will demonstrate this alteration.

"E♭" Major   "c" minor—Harmonic Form

Note:

1. The key signatures for "E♭" Major and its relative "c" minor are the same.
2. The "B♭" in the key signature is necessary in the major scale of "E♭" to provide the correct distance for "sol" in the key of "E♭."
3. The cancel is necessary to raise a note which had been previously flatted one half step.
4. "B" natural, the seventh note, is only one half step away from the key-note "c." Raising the seventh note creates a leading tone which gives a more definite feeling of finality once the keynote is reached.

The exercises provided for all harmonic scales should be completed before the third form of the minor scale is attempted. The procedure will be the same as that followed with the natural minor scale with these exceptions:

1. The seventh tone will be altered upward by one half step.
2. The selection of the proper chromatic sign is important.
3. To save time, simply raise the seventh tone of each of the previously written natural minor scales one half step.

Melodic Minor

The awkward distance of a step and a half between "fa" and "si" in the harmonic minor scale is changed through chromatic alteration in the melodic minor scale. This is accomplished by raising the pitch of "fa" one half step and assigning the Latin syllable "fi" to indicate this raised pitch. The distance between "fi" and "si" is one whole step rather than a step and a half as it is in the harmonic minor scale ("fa-si"). The practice of raising "fa" one half step to "fi" is used only in the ascending melodic minor scale. The descending melodic minor scale is the same as the natural minor scale.

Melodic Minor Scale Formula:

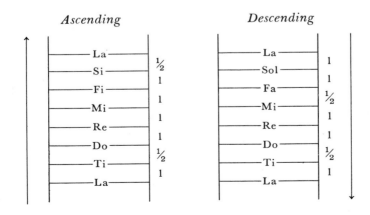

The descending scale should include chromatic signs to replace the chromatics which were added to create "fi" and "si." The cancel (♮) will remove the effect of a sharp or flat. On occasion, it will be necessary to restore a sharp or flat which was originally in the key signature. These had been removed by a cancel in the ascending form.

"a" Melodic Minor (Ascending)   "a" Melodic Minor (Descending)

la ti do re mi fi si la

la sol fa mi re do ti la

Note:

1. Whole step, "mi–fi" (E–F♯)
2. Whole step, "fi–si" (F♯–G♯)
3. Half step, "si–la" (G♯–A)
4. Half step, "ti–do" (B–C)

Note:

1. The cancel removes the effect of sharps on "fi" (F♯) and "si" (G♯) to create a natural minor form for the descending melodic minor scale.

2. The cancel in this case lowers the pitch of a note that had been previously raised by a sharp.

The example which follows will demonstrate the effect of the cancel, which raises the pitch of a note that has been previously lowered by a flat.

"E♭" Major   "c" minor—Melodic (Ascending and Descending)

do   la ti do re mi fi si la sol fa mi re do ti la

Note:

1. "E♭" major and its relative minor key, "c" minor (one and one half steps below "E♭" major) have the same key signature, three flats.
2. The cancel raises the sixth and seventh tones one half step. The cancel temporarily removes the flats on the second space and third line in the key signature. When you remove a flat with a cancel, the pitch is raised one half step.

3. The flats which were removed ascending the scale are restored in the descending scale, the natural minor form. Descending, the natural minor form must coincide with the key signature, which calls for "la" to "la" with no tones raised.

There are occasions when a scale tone is already sharped in the key signature and must be chromatically altered upward by one half step. In this case, the double sharp is used in the ascending melodic minor scale. Descending, one of the two sharps is removed by a cancel. The second sharp is a duplicate of the sharp on the same line or space in the key signature.

"B" Major   "G♯" Melodic Minor (Ascending and Descending)

Note:

1. "E" ("fa") is raised one half step to produce "fi."
2. "F" is double sharped to produce "si."
3. One of the two sharps on "F" is a duplicate of the "F♯" in the key signature.
4. The cancel removes one sharp, lowering the pitch one half step.
5. The remaining sharp is merely a reminder of the same sharp in the key signature.

The exercises provided for all melodic minor scales should be completed now. Due care should be exercised in the selection of the proper chromatic signs necessary to achieve the required alterations for the melodic minor scale.

CYCLE OF MINOR KEYS

Minor key signatures may be arranged as a cycle of keys having a pattern similar to that found in the Cycle of Major Keys.

Cycle of Minor Keys

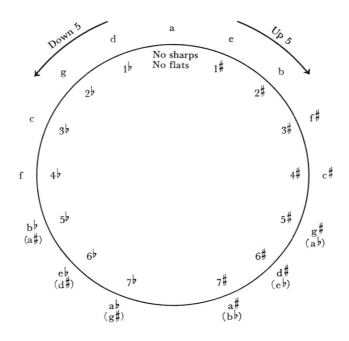

Note:

1. Reading clockwise are the sharp key signatures.
2. Counterclockwise are the flat key signatures.
3. Going clockwise, count up five letter names for each successive sharp key signature (upper dominants).
4. Going counterclockwise, count down five letter names for each successive flat key signature (subdominants or lower dominants).
5. Counting up seven half steps on the piano keyboard will establish the exact pitch name for each of the sharp key signatures in minor.
6. Counting down seven half steps on the piano keyboard will establish the exact pitch name for the flat key signatures in minor.

A cycle combining major keys and their relative minor keys having the same key signature will provide an instant reference for major-minor key relationships.

Cycle of Major Keys and Their Relative Minor Keys
(Having Same Key Signature)

Note:

Major keys—outside
Relative minor keys—inside

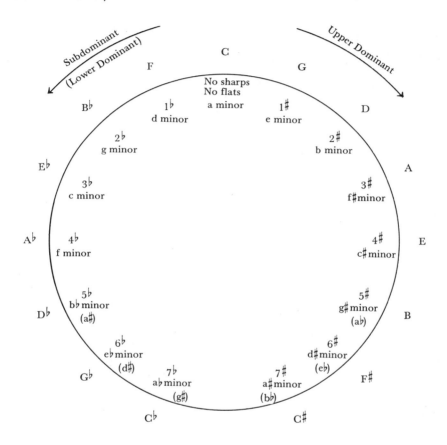

Note:

1. The keys in parentheses are enharmonic keys.
2. Going counterclockwise, the subdominant is also called the lower dominant, since it is five letter names below the previous key.
3. Going clockwise, the dominant is called the upper dominant, since it is five letter names above the previous key.
4. Counting seven half steps to the right on the piano keyboard will produce the exact pitch name for the next upper dominant.
5. Counting to the left seven half steps will produce the next subdominant.

TONIC MINOR

    Minor scales may be constructed on any given pitch without any direct attention applied to their relationship with a major key having the same key signature.

    The keynote of the "C" Major scale is "C" and this scale is produced by applying the whole and half step formula given for major scales. We can construct the three forms of any minor scale on any given pitch by placing the whole and half steps according to the formulas for each type of scale. The word "tonic" means that the pitch name of "C" provides the keynote (tonic) for "C" Major and also provides the keynote (tonic) for "c" minor. The pitch of "C" will indicate the starting note for the four scales which follow.

"C" Major

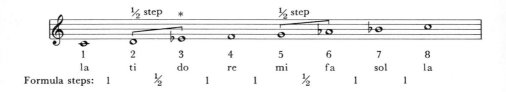

"c" minor—Natural

"c" minor—Harmonic

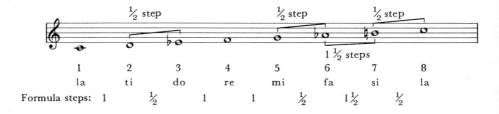

"c" minor—Melodic (Ascending)

½ step	*		1 step		½ step

1 step

1	2	3	4	5	6	7	8
la	ti	do	re	mi	fi	si	la

Formula steps: 1   ½   1   1   1   1   ½

"c" minor—Melodic (Descending)

*

½ step   ½ step

8	7	6	5	4	3	2	1
la	sol	fa	mi	re	do	ti	la

Formula steps: 1   1   ½   1   1   ½   1

Note: The third note in each of the three forms of the minor scale is the same—lowered one half step from the third note in major.

Exercises

Natural Minor

1. Construct a cycle of major key signatures. Within the cycle show the pitch name for each relative minor key.

2. Build a natural minor scale for each relative major key having the same key signature.

Harmonic Minor

To create the harmonic form of the minor scales, add the proper chromatic sign to the seventh note of the natural minor scales constructed previously.

Melodic Minor

To create the ascending melodic form of the minor scales, simply add the proper chromatic sign to the sixth note of the harmonic minor scale constructed previously. Each ascending form should be followed by a descending form, which will be the equivalent of the natural minor for each key.

Note: The replacement or addition of chromatic signs is a typical feature of the descending form of the melodic minor scales.

Tonic Minor

1. Build natural minor scales on the tonic (keynote) minors of E♭, D, B.

2.   Build harmonic minor scales on the tonic minors of E, G, Bb.

3.   Build melodic minor scales, ascending and descending, on the
     tonic minors of C, F, F#.

chapter

7

MORE

SCALES

In addition to the various major and minor scale forms commonly used, there are other scale forms which provide variety and color. The chromatic scale is one example.

CHROMATIC SCALE

The chromatic scale is made up exclusively of half steps. There are Latin syllables assigned to each note of the major scale and also to each note of the chromatic scale. The musical ladder below shows the syllables for the major scales on the ladder. The half steps above and below the major scale steps are shown on the outside of the ladder. These half steps are called "chromatics," alterations of scale tones. A combination of scale tones and chromatic tones makes up the chromatic scale. To read up the chromatic scale, we read from the center out to the right in a zigzag manner. Reading down, we read from the center out to the left also in a zigzag manner.

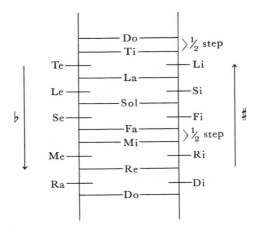

Note: The major scale already has a half step between "mi"–"fa" and "ti"–"do." It is not necessary to go outside the ladder, since "mi" raised one half step becomes "fa." "Fa" lowered one half step becomes "mi." In this case, the same syllable is used for this half step in the major scale and in the chromatic scale. The same is true for "ti"–"do," which is one half step in the major scale. "Ti" raised one half step becomes "do." The same syllable is used for this half step in both the major scale and the chromatic scale. "Do" lowered one half step becomes "ti."

Chromatic Scale with Syllables and Notes (Ascending)

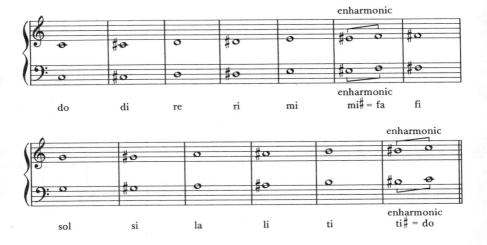

Note:

1. The sharp chromatic (♯) is used to raise each scale tone one half step.
2. There are seven different major scale notes.
3. There are only five real chromatic changes, since the two additional chromatics are enharmonic equivalents.

Chromatic Scale with Syllables and Notes (Descending)

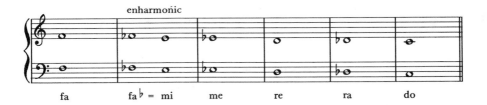

Note:

1. The flat chromatic (♭) is used to lower each scale tone one half step.
2. There are seven different major scale notes.
3. There are only five real chromatic changes, since the two additional chromatics are enharmonic equivalents.
4. C up to B on the piano keyboard is seven white keys with five black keys between them. The combined total represents twelve half steps.

The chromatic scale actually encompasses twelve consecutive half steps.

The following example shows the notes of the ascending "C" Major scale enclosed with brackets.

Chromatic Scale (Ascending)

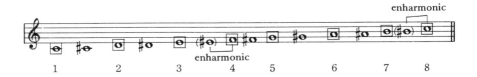

Between each note of the "C" Major scale is a chromatic sign (♯), which creates one half step. The whole steps found in the major scale are now divided into two half steps. The half steps in the major scale between three and four and seven and eight are already present. However, the third and seventh notes must be altered chromatically in order to be technically correct in showing the half step arrangement. In other words, each note of the ascending "C" Major scale is followed by one chromatic alteration on the same line or space except for three and four and seven and eight, which are already one half step apart. The above example shows the ascending form using the sharp chromatic to create one half step above each note of the ascending "C" Major scale. The combined result becomes the ascending form of the chromatic scale starting on C.

Note: The enharmonic equivalents between 3–4 and 7–8 are enclosed in brackets to indicate the half steps already present. Since F is the next half step above E, the E♯ is not necessary. The B♯ is not necessary, since the "C" is the next half step above "B."

The following example presents the descending form of the chromatic scale starting on C.

Chromatic Scale (Descending)

Again, the "C" Major scale notes are enclosed with brackets. The enharmonic equivalents at eight—seven and four—three are enclosed in parentheses. Each note of the descending "C" Major scale is followed by one chromatic alteration on the same line or space.

In this case, the flat chromatic is used to make one half step below each note of the descending major scale. The combined result becomes the descending form of the chromatic scale starting on C.

WHOLE TONE SCALE

The whole tone scale is different from the traditional major and minor scales in that it contains only six tones rather than the seven found in the majors and minors (the eighth note in major and minor is merely a duplicate of the keynote to complete the octave). Another difference lies in the use of whole tone steps exclusively, rather than whole and half steps. The resulting sound is modern and gives an elusive feeling rather than a strong tendency toward a keynote. This may be accounted for by the absence of a leading tone.

To gain a sense of the unique sound of the whole tone scale, the student is advised to try the following whole tone scale pattern on the piano. Depress the sustaining pedal so that the notes will continue to sound and then play this whole tone scale.

C   D   E   F♯   G♯   A♯   C

Note:

1. The whole tone scale does not follow the consecutive line-space arrangement of the major-minor system. There is a skip between the fifth and sixth steps.
2. The complete whole tone scale is encountered frequently but fragments are also used for certain effects.

An incomplete portion of this scale can be played easily by the five fingers of the right hand. Keep the sustaining pedal down and play the notes rapidly at first in the high register of the piano. Gradually slow down and let them fade out. Imagine the effect of throwing a pebble into a quiet brook. The water eddies rapidly at first and then gradually subsides. The effect resembles the impressionism of Debussy.

* The seventh tone of the scale is merely a repetition of the first tone.

This is a typical sound for a pattern of whole tones. This grouping has five of the six tones of the complete whole tone scale. Add D to this group and the whole tone scale is complete.

Whole tone scales can be constructed on any of the seven basic white keys or the five black keys. Remember to use chromatics where necessary to create the whole steps.

Note: The whole tone scale does not follow the consecutive line-space arrangement of the major-minor system but has a skip between the fifth and sixth steps on the staff.

The exercises for whole tone scales should be completed before attempting the next type of scale.

PENTATONIC SCALE

The pentatonic scale is a five-tone scale which had its origin in antiquity. Its special sound has intrigued many composers in the twentieth century. Debussy, for instance, used this scale as the basis for one of his compositions, "The Maid With the Flaxen Hair" ("La fille aux cheveux de lin").[1]

Some remnants of this scale are reputed to be in evidence in the mountain regions of China. A sample of the Oriental effect of the pentatonic scale may be obtained by playing on the five black keys in the upper register. Try to approximate a Chinese-type melody and the sound of the pentatonic scale will register in your hearing.

[1] Published by Durand & Cie, Paris, Elkan-Vogel, Inc., sole agents in U.S.A.

The music of the American Indian contains elements of the pentatonic scale. Try improvising a war chant using only the five black keys in the lower register of the piano. There was at one time an interesting theory about the origin of the American Indian. Musicologists pointed to the presence of the ancient pentatonic scale in the music of the American Indian; anthropologists pointed to his facial structure. On the basis of these observations, it was suggested that the American Indians were in fact the lost tribe of Israel. Although this has not been substantiated, it is an interesting theory, since music is a true recording of any society in the history of man and it travels when man travels.

There are two basic forms of the pentatonic scale. The first one will parallel the arrangement of black keys on the piano keyboard, starting with the group of two black keys followed by three black keys. The formula for this arrangement is as follows:

step—step and one half—step—step

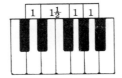

This formula may be applied to black keys or white keys. Starting on Middle C, this arrangement of the pentatonic scale would be:

It is interesting to note that many Irish and Scottish folk songs are based on the pentatonic scale. Like the whole tone scale, there is no leading tone, which contributes to its elusive sound. The pentatonic scale is also a favorite of jazz musicians in their improvisations.

The Scottish folk song "Loch Lomond" is based on this first formula of the pentatonic scale.

LOCH LOMOND

Scotland

The second form of the pentatonic scale will parallel another arrangement of the black keys on the piano keyboard, starting with the group of three black keys followed by two black keys. The formula for this arrangement is as follows:

step—step—step and one half—step

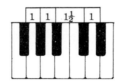

This formula may be applied to black keys or white keys. Starting on Middle C, this arrangement of the pentatonic would be:

The Irish folk song "Down By the Sally Gardens" uses this arrangement of the pentatonic scale.

DOWN BY THE SALLY GARDENS

Ireland

From *Irish Country Songs,* Vol. I. Copyright 1909 by Boosey & Co., Ltd.; re-newed 1936. Reprinted by permission of Boosey & Hawkes, Inc.

The exercises assigned for the pentatonic scale will complete our work with scales.

Exercises

1. Write an ascending and descending chromatic scale on the pitch of C on the Grand Staff.

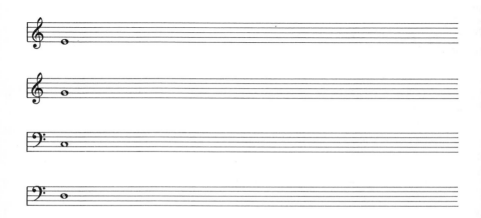

2. Sound the pitch for Middle C on the piano, and slowly sing the chromatic scale up and down using the correct Latin syllables. Play each note as you sing. Gradually eliminate the piano as you sing except to check the pitch at various points.

Whole Tone Scale

1. Build whole tone scales based on the given notes:

2. a. Sing a whole tone scale starting on Middle C using the neutral syllable "loo." Use the piano at first and then gradually eliminate it from your practice.

    b. Start on other keys which are in your voice range and repeat this procedure.

Pentatonic Scale

1. Write pentatonic scales on the following pitches:

2. Sing pentatonic scales using the syllable "loo" on various pitches.

3. Compose an eight measure folk song based on the notes of the pentatonic scale.

chapter

8

INTERVALS

An interval is the measurement in pitch between any two tones. Intervals may be melodic, in which case the two tones sound one after the other,

or harmonic when they sound simultaneously.

    Intervals have numerical names which are determined by the size of the interval. The basic intervals found in all major scales are shown first with the Latin syllable names.

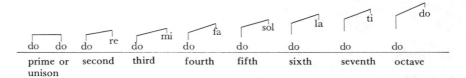

Shown on the Grand Staff are the melodic intervals for the "C" Major scale:

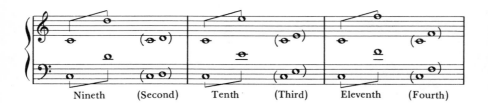

Intervals are measured from the bottom note, which may be considered as the keynote. If the upper note of the interval is in the major scale of the lower note, the interval is major or perfect. Perfect refers to fourths, fifths, octaves, and unisons.

Intervals exceeding the octave are called compound intervals and are in fact extended forms of lesser intervals. Compound intervals and their smaller equivalents are:

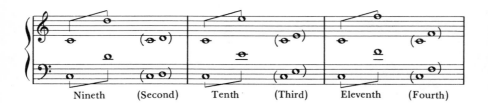

To quickly determine any compound interval merely add seven to the smaller interval; to a second add seven and the compound result is a ninth; to a third add seven and the result is a tenth; to a fourth add seven and the result is an eleventh; to a fifth add seven and the result is a twelfth; to a sixth add seven and the result is a thirteenth.

In addition to the numerical names assigned to each interval, there are more specific names added to further define the exact nature of the interval. Intervals are qualified by the terms consonant, dissonant, perfect, imperfect, major, minor, augmented, or diminished.

Originally, only the intervals of unison (prime), octave, fourth, and fifth were allowed, since they were considered consonant or pleasant-sounding. These intervals are called perfect intervals. The term "perfect" is derived from the computations provided by the Greek mathematician Pythagoras in the sixth century B.C. His ratios for these intervals were:

Perfect Interval	Ratio
Octave	2:1
Fifth	3:2
Fourth	4:3

Every musical tone that is produced is a combination of a strong tone, which is heard as a pitch, and a series of weaker tones, which reverberate sympathetically over the pitch. These weaker tones, which are called overtones, make a contribution to the overall quality of the tone heard as a pitch. The overtones occur in a series which is designated numerically. The largest intervals in the overtone series are the lowest in pitch. As they ascend, the intervals become smaller.

Overtone Series

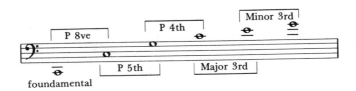

Note that the perfect intervals are the lowest in the series. The original sanctity of the perfect intervals may be due to the fact that they are the most fundamental in the overtone series.

A detailed explanation of the arithmetical calculations for the ratios of all intervals may be found in the *Harvard Dictionary of Music*.[1] For our purpose at this point, a simpler explanation will suffice. In the Middle Ages the hollow sounds of octaves, fourths, and fifths were the intervals considered consonant or pleasant to the ear. To our ears they tend to sound hollow and archaic. They do represent in sound, how-

---

[1] Willi Apel, *Harvard Dictionary of Music,* rev. ed. (Cambridge, Mass.: Harvard University Press, 1969).

ever, the vastness and hollow effect of the Gothic cathedrals. The prime, fourth, fifth, and octave are called perfect consonances and are labeled:

> Perfect prime
> Perfect fourth
> Perfect fifth
> Perfect octave

Actually, only the unison and octave are considered to be mathematically consonant. We find consonance to be a relative concept depending upon who is listening and which period of music history is involved.

The intervals of the third and sixth are called imperfect consonances. These intervals were originally considered less acceptable to the ear. They were finally given some status as consonances by the English composer John Dunstable in the early fifteenth century. To our ears, a succession of thirds and sixths tends to be somewhat saccharine.

Opposed to the perfect and imperfect consonances are the so-called dissonances. Here again we are dealing with a matter of individual preference. The sounds one listener will consider harsh, another will find acceptable. Rather than define dissonance as harshness, it would appear more practical to relate dissonance to the degree of restless energy contained in any combination of tones. A high degree may be considered dissonant. Conversely, then, consonance would be considered relatively at rest and lacking in restless energy. These definitions seem better for modern music. The dissonant intervals are the second and seventh of the scale, as well as augmented and diminished intervals.

In nontechnical language, all types of intervals may be described by their overall quality or color.

Interval	Quality or Color
Major	Bright
Minor	Dark, melancholic
Perfect	Hollow
Augmented	Vivid, modern, reaching outward
Diminished	Very dark, depressed, reaching inward
Consonant	Relatively at rest
Dissonant	Displaying restless energy

From the discussion on consonance and dissonance we now turn to the calculations and naming of all intervals.

INTERVALLIC STEPS

Counting the whole and half steps on the piano keyboard will determine the exact distance for any given interval. The following intervals of the "C" Major scale will be analyzed so that this knowledge may be applied to all major scales.

Major Scale

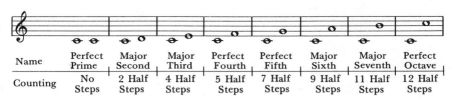

Name	Perfect Prime	Major Second	Major Third	Perfect Fourth	Perfect Fifth	Major Sixth	Major Seventh	Perfect Octave
Counting	No Steps	2 Half Steps	4 Half Steps	5 Half Steps	7 Half Steps	9 Half Steps	11 Half Steps	12 Half Steps

The following intervallic steps of the "a" minor scale in its three forms will be the same for all minor scales in related forms.

Natural Minor

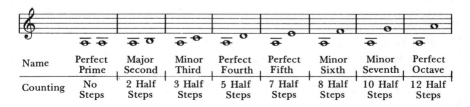

Name	Perfect Prime	Major Second	Minor Third	Perfect Fourth	Perfect Fifth	Minor Sixth	Minor Seventh	Perfect Octave
Counting	No Steps	2 Half Steps	3 Half Steps	5 Half Steps	7 Half Steps	8 Half Steps	10 Half Steps	12 Half Steps

Harmonic Minor

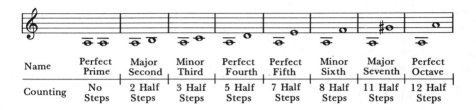

Name	Perfect Prime	Major Second	Minor Third	Perfect Fourth	Perfect Fifth	Minor Sixth	Major Seventh	Perfect Octave
Counting	No Steps	2 Half Steps	3 Half Steps	5 Half Steps	7 Half Steps	8 Half Steps	11 Half Steps	12 Half Steps

Note that the only difference between the natural minor and the harmonic minor is the raised seventh tone (leading tone) of the harmonic minor. This alteration upward from ten half steps to eleven makes a major seventh.

Melodic Minor

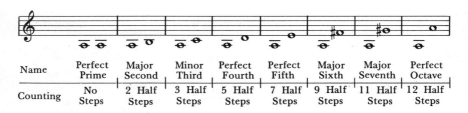

Name	Perfect Prime	Major Second	Minor Third	Perfect Fourth	Perfect Fifth	Major Sixth	Major Seventh	Perfect Octave
Counting	No Steps	2 Half Steps	3 Half Steps	5 Half Steps	7 Half Steps	9 Half Steps	11 Half Steps	12 Half Steps

Note that both the sixth and seventh steps are raised one half step, which creates the intervals of a major sixth and a major seventh.

Intervals may be perfect, major, or minor, as we have discovered in our study so far. They may also be augmented or diminished. Augmented intervals generally are the result of expanding major intervals or perfect intervals by one half step. An example of this may be found in the "fa" to "si" of the harmonic minor scale, which is an augmented second interval. A major second is two half steps ("fa" to "sol"); three half steps make the augmented second interval ("fa" to "si").

Major intervals become minor by reducing the major interval by one half step. Conversely, minor intervals expanded by one half step become major. Diminished intervals are produced by shrinking by one half step a perfect interval or a minor interval. Diminished intervals raised one half step become minor or perfect.

The following table will show how intervals change their character through chromatic alteration.

The student is reminded that:

A ♯ will raise a scale tone one half step;

A ♭ will lower a scale tone one half step;

A ♮ will remove the effect of a ♭ on a note, thereby raising the note one half step;

A ♮ will remove the effect of a ♯ on a note, thereby lowering the note one half step.

Additionally, a double sharp written ♯♯ or ✗ will raise a note two half steps.

A double flat (♭♭) will lower a note by two half steps.

TABLE XI: INTERVAL CHANGES

	Major	Minor	Perfect	Augmented	Diminished
Raised one half step	Augmented	Major	Augmented	Doubly Augmented*	Minor (or perfect if fourth, fifth, eighth, or prime is involved)
Lowered one half step	Minor	Diminished	Diminished	Major (or perfect if fourth, fifth eighth, or prime is involved)	Doubly Diminished*
Raised two half steps	Doubly Augmented*	Augmented	Doubly Augmented*		
Lowered two half steps	Diminished	Doubly Diminished*	Doubly Diminished*	Minor (or diminished if fourth, fifth, eighth, or prime is involved)	Rewritten as an enharmonic equivalent*

* These changes are more theoretical than practical and may be presented more effectively through the utilization of enharmonic spellings. This will simplify the written versions of some doubly augmented and doubly diminished intervals.

The combination of ♮♯ indicates that one sharp is to be retained (usually the one in the key signature), while the second sharp is cancelled.

The same is true of ♮♭. One flat is retained (usually in the key signature), and the second flat is cancelled.

Attention is drawn to the function of the double flat (♭♭) and the double sharp (♯♯ or ✕) in doubly diminished and doubly augmented intervals.

Enharmonic Equivalents

| Doubly Diminished Fifth | = | Perfect Fourth | Doubly Augmented Fifth | = | Major Sixth |

Doubly diminished and doubly augmented intervals produce enharmonic equivalents.

It is interesting to note that raising the upper tone in an interval makes that interval larger. Conversely, lowering the lower tone will produce the same size interval.

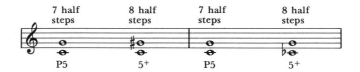

| 7 half steps | 8 half steps | 7 half steps | 8 half steps |
| P5 | 5⁺ | P5 | 5⁺ |

Place your hands above each other about a foot apart for the perfect fifth ———. Raise the upper hand for the augmented fifth. Return to the position for the perfect fifth. Now lower the bottom hand. This also produces an augmented fifth, since the distance in both cases is larger than the perfect fifth. Although the flat is lowered a tone, the actual size of the interval is increased. This is true of all intervals.

The intervals presented next show the interval names abbreviated for simplicity:

Capital M   = Major
Small m   = Minor
Capital P   = Perfect
Capital P 1   = Perfect Prime
Plus sign +   = Augmented
Small zero ₀ = Diminished

Twenty Seven Intervals

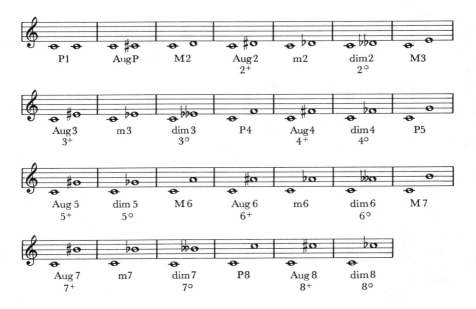

ENHARMONIC INTERVALS

To acquire a knowledge of the enharmonic spelling of intervals, the best approach is through the piano keyboard. Remember that every black key has two names. In the context of an ascending progression it will be considered as an upward chromatic of its nearest white key to the

left 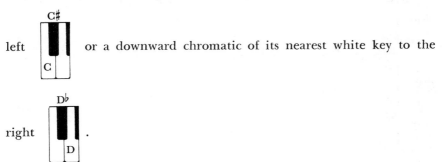 or a downward chromatic of its nearest white key to the

right .

In other words, the same black key is involved in both cases. C♯ and D♭, therefore, are enharmonic equivalents. It may be more practical on occasion to write certain complex intervals in their enharmonic form.

Enharmonic Equivalents

Example:

$$G\sharp = A\flat$$

$$\frac{C\sharp}{P\,5} = \frac{D\flat}{P\,5}$$

Sharps ↑

C♯ = D♭	C♭ = B
D♯ = E♭	D♭ = C♯
E♯ = F	E♭ = D♯
F♯ = G♭	F♭ = E
G♯ = A♭	G♭ = F♯
A♯ = B♭	A♭ = G♯
B♯ = C	B♭ = A♯

Flats ↓

The summary of intervals which is presented next indicates the number of half steps in each specific interval.

Summary of Intervals

INVERSION OF INTERVALS

When intervals are inverted, the new interval produced is the opposite in effect of the original interval except in the case of perfect intervals. Perfect intervals inverted remain perfect, although the size of the interval changes. The inversions of intervals result in:

> Perfect inverting to perfect
> Major inverting to minor
> Minor inverting to major
> Augmented inverting to diminished
> Diminished inverting to augmented

Although a perfect interval inverted remains perfect, the size of the interval is different. Consequently, a different interval, also perfect, is the result.

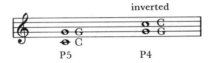

The example showing $\overset{G}{\underset{P5}{C}}$ has C acting as the keynote or 1. The lower note of each interval is treated as an individual major keynote. Therefore, C on the bottom of the interval indicates "C" Major with C as 1. The inversion has G on the bottom, which makes G the keynote (1), and C now becomes 4 in "G" Major. Both notes occur in both keys, making a perfect interval.

The octave inverted remains the same, an octave.

A simple way in which to determine the size of the new interval is to subtract the size of the old interval from nine.

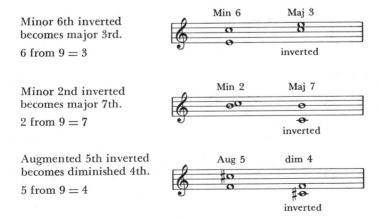

Minor 6th inverted becomes major 3rd.

6 from 9 = 3

Minor 2nd inverted becomes major 7th.

2 from 9 = 7

Augmented 5th inverted becomes diminished 4th.

5 from 9 = 4

Although this is a fifth inverted to a fourth, the two intervals are not perfect but rather augmented inverted to diminished.

IDENTIFYING SPECIFIC INTERVALS

In order to label any interval perfect, major, minor, augmented, or diminished, it is necessary to know the number of half steps in each interval. If the upper note of the interval is in the major scale of the lower note, we merely decide which one of the scale steps it is (second, third, fourth, fifth, sixth, seventh, eighth) and name it. The scale steps are derived from the major keynote, which is the lower note of the interval.

 6th

The upper tone A is in the scale of "C" Major. The result, then, is a major sixth with nine half steps.

If the upper note is not in the major scale of the lower note, we then decide whether it is basically a second, third, fourth, fifth, sixth, seventh, or eighth. Is it higher or lower than the original scale tone? How much? For instance, a half step up on perfect intervals produces an augmented interval.

 Aug 5th

The fifth note in the scale of "C" is G. Here we have a G♯. C to G is a perfect fifth (five half steps). A perfect fifth raised one half step becomes an augmented fifth (six half steps).

In working with intervals it is important to remember that it is the distance between the two notes which creates the specific name of each interval. For instance, in the following examples, the intervals are made smaller or larger in two ways: by expanding or reducing the upper tone or by expanding or reducing the lower tone.

In this example we have achieved the same sized intervals through the expansion or reduction of the distance in each one. This can be verified by checking the half steps in each case on the piano. The sharp does not always produce an augmented interval. When it is placed before the lower note in any interval, it actually shrinks the distance between the two notes of the interval, thereby reducing the size of the interval by one half step. A similar condition exists when using flats. A flat can make the interval larger by lowering the lower tone. A flat on the upper tone, however, reduces the size of the interval.

Intervals must be heard within a key in order for us to assign a specific name to any one interval. An interval that is three half steps in size could be a minor third. It could also be an augmented second. Out of context (key) we cannot determine the spelling of the interval any more than we could decide how to spell "their/there" without the context of the sentence.

The following have the same sound out of context:

1. Augmented seconds and minor thirds = three half steps
2. Major thirds and diminished fourths = four half steps
3. Augmented fourths and diminished fifths = six half steps

Exercises

1. Identify by specific names (perfect, major, minor) the intervals found in the major scale:

2. Give the compound name and the smaller equivalent name for each of the following intervals:

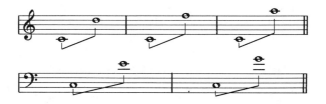

3. Write two examples of imperfect consonances in the key of "C" Major.

4. Write two examples of dissonant intervals in the key of "C" Major.

5. Indicate the number of half steps in each interval of the major scale.

Name								
Number of half steps								

6. Give the specific name for each interval (perfect, major, minor, augmented, or diminished) found in the three forms of the minor scale and show the number of half steps in each interval.

"a" Natural Minor

Interval Name								
Number of half steps								

"*a*" Harmonic Minor

Interval Name								
Number of half steps								

"*a*" Melodic Minor

Interval Name								
Number of half steps								

7. Identify the following intervals as perfect, major, minor, augmented, or diminished. Use the abbreviations given for intervals:

A.

B.

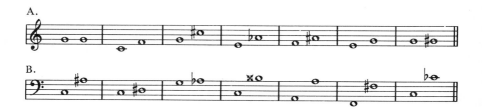

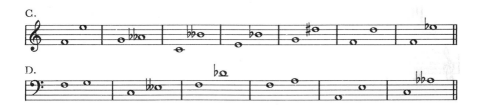

8. Write the enharmonic equivalent for each note.

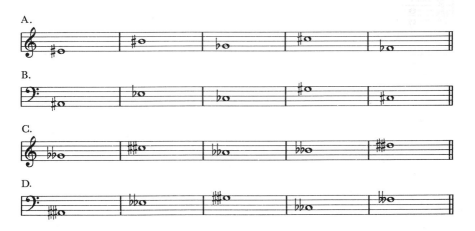

9. Show the enharmonic equivalents for each of these intervals:

10.   Invert the following intervals and name the specific interval produced.

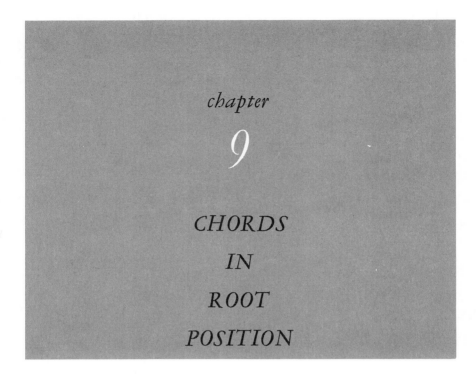

chapter 9

CHORDS IN ROOT POSITION

The combination of two or more intervals of a third sounding together or in succession is referred to as a chord. Since intervals are the elements of a chord, it is logical to find that chords are also divided into four types: major, minor, augmented, and diminished.

A chord consisting of two intervals of a third is more specifically called a triad. In analyzing a triad in root position, we find that the lowest note to the highest is the interval of a fifth, which may be perfect, augmented, or diminished. The piano keyboard will verify the half steps.

Perfect Fifth

7 half steps = P5

This interval may also be

Augmented Fifth

8 half steps = 5⁺

or

Diminished Fifth

6 half steps = 5°

The remaining note of the triad, which is the middle note, is the interval of a third above the lowest note of the triad and the interval of a third below the highest note of the triad.

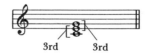

3rd   3rd

These two thirds may be major or minor, and it is interesting to see what happens to the quality of the triad depending upon the size of the two intervals involved.

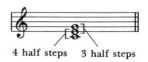

4 half steps   3 half steps

Lower interval   4 half steps = major third
Upper interval   3 half steps = minor third

Rule: When a triad consists of a major third on the bottom and a minor third on top, the result is a *major triad*.

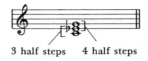

3 half steps   4 half steps

Lower interval   3 half steps = minor third
Upper interval   4 half steps = major third

Rule: A minor third on the bottom and a major third on top = a *minor triad.*

4 half steps   4 half steps

Lower interval   4 half steps = major third
Upper interval   4 half steps = major third

Rule: A major third on bottom and a major third on top = an *augmented triad.*

3 half steps   3 half steps

Lower interval   3 half steps = minor third
Upper interval   3 half steps = minor third

Rule: A minor third on the bottom and a minor third on top = a *diminished triad.*

Each note of the scale has a unique function insofar as chords are concerned. Each note of the scale serves as the root of a specific chord and has a name indicative of its function. The piano keyboard should be utilized in building the correct intervals for each chord.

TONIC CHORD (Triad) IN "C" MAJOR

The tonic chord is based on the first note in the scale ("do"). The first note ("do") of the scale is represented by the Arabic numeral 1.

Scale Tone Symbol—"Do"

When we refer to the chord based on the first note of the scale (tonic chord), we use the Roman numeral I.

Tonic Chord Symbol

If the Roman numeral is capitalized (I), the chord is major or augmented. The plus sign indicates an augmented chord.

Capitalized—Major or Augmented

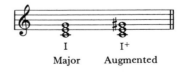

If the Roman numeral is not capitalized (i), it is minor or diminished. The small zero indicates a diminished chord.

Non-Capitalized—Minor or Diminished

The use of capitalized or non-capitalized Roman numerals is optional, but they do provide a quick method of recognition for the quality of a chord.

CHORDS ON THE MAJOR SCALE

Arabic Numerals

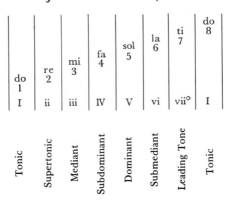

The chords using any of these scale tones as roots will be expressed in either capitalized or non-capitalized Roman numerals depending upon the size and position of the intervals in each chord. Special names are assigned to the root of each chord to indicate which note of the scale is involved.

Major Scale Chord Symbols

"C" Major Root Position Chords

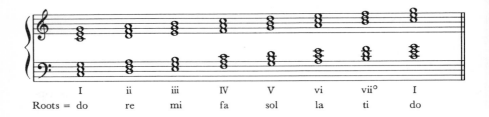

	I	ii	iii	IV	V	vi	vii°	I
Roots =	do	re	mi	fa	sol	la	ti	do

From the foregoing we learn that:

The   I   IV   and   V   chords are

root = do   root = fa   root = sol
(tonic)   (subdominant)   (dominant)

major since they have an interval of a major third on the bottom (4 half steps) and an interval of a minor third on the top (3 half steps).

ii, iii and vi are minor (minor third on bottom, major third on top). Root = re, mi, and la.

vii° is diminished (minor third on bottom, minor third on top). Root = ti.

CHORDS ON MINOR SCALES

Arabic Numerals
Natural Minor

The chords using any of these scale tones as roots will be expressed in either capitalized or non-capitalized Roman numerals depending upon the size and position of the intervals in each chord.

Minor Scale

							la 8
						sol 7	
					fa 6		
				mi 5			
			re 4				
		do 3					
	ti 2						
la 1							
i	ii°	III	iv	v	VI	VII	i

"a" Natural Minor Root Position Chords

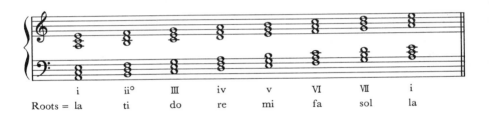

i	ii°	III	iv	v	VI	VII	i
Roots = la	ti	do	re	mi	fa	sol	la

It is now apparent that in the natural minor:

i, iv and v are minor;

III, VI and VII are major;

ii° is diminished.

Harmonic Minor Scale

la
1

ti
2

do
3

re
4

mi
5

fa
6

si
7 ← raised

la
8

"a" Harmonic Minor

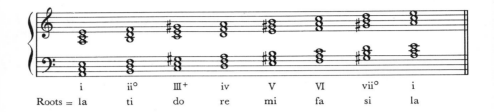

i	ii°	III+	iv	V	VI	vii°	i
Roots = la	ti	do	re	mi	fa	si	la

In the harmonic minor we find:

i and iv are minor;

V and VI are major (sol♯, changes size of intervals);

ii° and vii° are diminished;

III+ is augmented (sol♯, [si] changes size of intervals).

Melodic Minor Scale

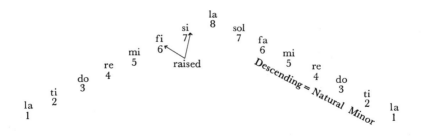

Ascending

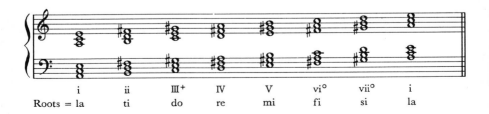

i	ii	III+	IV	V	vi°	vii°	i
Roots = la	ti	do	re	mi	fi	si	la

Descending

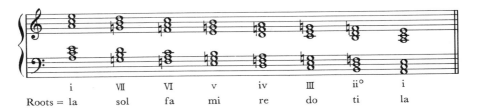

	i	VII	VI	v	iv	III	ii°	i
Roots =	la	sol	fa	mi	re	do	ti	la

The changes in the melodic minor scale merit close attention, since the corresponding chords involve more detail because of the chromatic alteration.

In the melodic minor:

Ascending:

 i and ii are minor;
 IV and V are major;
 vi° and vii° are diminished;
 III+ is augmented;

Descending:

 i, iv, and v are minor;
 III, VI, and VII are major;
 ii° is diminished.

Remember:

1. You must take into account the sharps or flats in each new key signature when counting the steps in each prescribed interval.
2. All the steps for measuring the intervals in "C" Major will be the same for all other major keys. Only the letter names and position of the first tone on the piano will be different.
3. The steps for measuring the intervals in all three forms of the "a" minor scale will be the same for the three forms of all other minor keys. Only the letter names and position of the first tone on the piano will be different.
4. Major: I ii iii IV V vi vii° I.
5. Natural minor: i ii° III iv v VI VII i.
6. Harmonic minor: i ii° III+ iv V VI vii° i.
7. Melodic minor:
 (ascending) i ii III+ IV V vi° vii° .i.
 (descending) i VII VI v iv III ii° i.
8. Triads in root position will have all three notes on lines or all three notes on spaces.

Augmented Triads (Two Major Thirds)

Diminished Triads (Two Minor Thirds)

The student is advised to work with triads as follows:

1. Review basic intervals using the piano keyboard as a guide.
2. Review the intervals found in the triads of the "C" Major scale. (Remember that these intervals are the same size in all major keys.)
3. Review the intervals found in the triads of the natural form of the "a" minor scale. (Remember that these intervals are the same size in all natural minor scales.)
4. Review the intervals found in the triads of the "a" minor scale, harmonic form. (Remember that these intervals are the same size in all harmonic minor scales.)
5. Review the intervals found in the triads of the "a" minor scale, melodic form, ascending and descending. (Remember that these intervals are the same size in all melodic minor scales.)

Exercises

In these exercises there are several things to be done:

1. Identify the key (if minor, give the form).
2. Label all triads as major, minor, augmented, or diminished with Roman numerals.
3. Write the correct Latin syllables next to each note in every triad.
4. Write the correct Arabic numerals next to each note to indicate which scale tones are included.

Note: All chords are in root position and have been chosen more or less at random in each key since identification is our primary purpose at this point. Chromatic alteration will indicate some of the minor keys.

24.

25.

Write augmented triads based on these roots:

35.

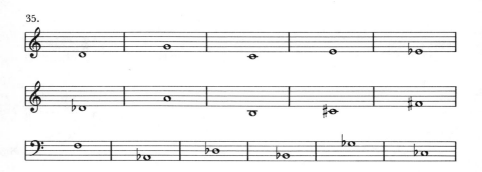

Write diminished triads based on these roots:

36.

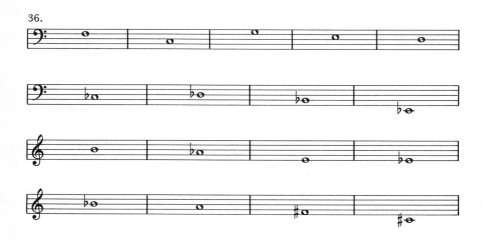

chapter

10

CHORDS

IN

INVERSION

MAJOR KEYS

All chords have a number of positions or arrangements of their tones which are equal to the number of tones in each chord. A three-note chord (triad) will have three positions. A four-note chord will have four positions.

The basic or first position of any chord is called "root" position. As we have learned, root position means that the scale tone on which the chord is built is the bottom note of the chord.

"C" Major—Root Position

Tonic Chord

Note:

1　Root of the chord ("do") is on the bottom.
3　Third of the chord ("mi") is in the middle.
5　Fifth of the chord ("sol") is on the top.

The second position of any chord is called "first inversion." To obtain a first inversion of any chord we merely move up to the next note of the chord and the root now goes to the top of the chord.

"C" Major—First Inversion

Tonic Chord

Note:

3　Third of the chord ("mi") is on the bottom.
5　Fifth of the chord ("sol") is in the middle.
1　Root of the chord ("do") is on the top.

The Roman numeral I indicates a tonic chord. The Arabic 6 attached to it indicates the first inversion of the tonic chord. For that matter, the Arabic 6 attached to any chord symbol will represent a first inversion of the chord (IV6, iii6, vi6, V6).

The Arabic 6 also represents the size of the interval between the lowest and highest notes.

Interval of a Sixth—"C" Major

Tonic Chord

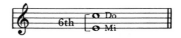

The third position of any chord is called "second inversion." To obtain the second inversion of any chord we move up to the next note of the chord; the root now is in the middle of the chord.

"C" Major—Second Inversion

Tonic Chord

I_4^6

Note:

1. The I means tonic chord is major.
2. The 6 means that the interval between the lowest and highest notes is a sixth.
3. The 4 means that the interval between the lowest and middle notes is a fourth.

The   attached to any chord symbol means a second inversion of the chord. (I_4^6, IV_4^6, V_4^6)

MINOR KEYS

"a" Minor—Root Position

Tonic Chord

i

Note:

1   Root of the tonic minor chord ("la") is on the bottom.
3   Third of the chord ("do") is on the bottom.
5   Fifth of the chord ("mi") is on the top.
i   Tonic chord is in root position in minor.

"a" Minor—First Inversion

Tonic Chord

Note:

3   Third of the chord ("do") is on the bottom.
5   Fifth of the chord ("mi") is in the middle.
1   Root of the chord ("la") is on the top.
i6 Tonic chord is in first inversion in minor.

The 6 means that the interval of a sixth exists between the lowest and highest notes.

"a" Minor—Second Inversion

Tonic Chord

Note:

1. The i indicates a tonic chord in minor.
2. The 6 indicates that the interval between the lowest and highest notes is a sixth.
3. The 4 indicates that the interval between the lowest and middle notes is a fourth.
4. The $^6_4$ attached to any chord symbol indicates a second inversion of the chord. (i$^6_4$, iv$^6_4$, V$^6_4$, etc.)

The three positions of the triadic chords based on the notes of the "C" major scale are:

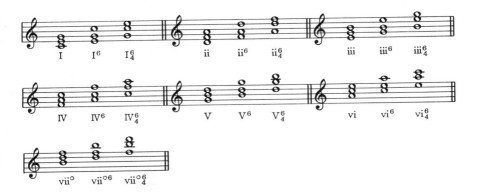

Once the keynote ("do") is established, this process can be repeated in all major keys.

The three positions based on the notes of the "a" minor scale in the natural form are:

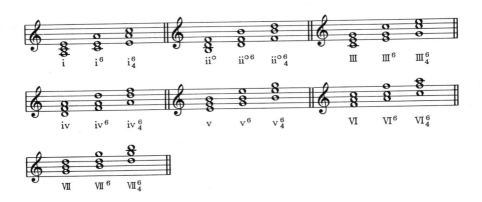

Once the keynote ("la") for the minor scale is established, this process can be used for all minor keys.

The harmonic and melodic forms of the minor keys will involve some chromatic alterations. These alterations will change the size of some intervals in a chord. The change in the intervals will be indicated by the Roman numerals.

"a" Harmonic Minor

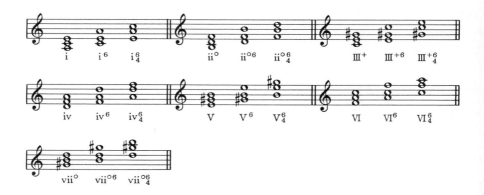

"a" Melodic Minor (Ascending)

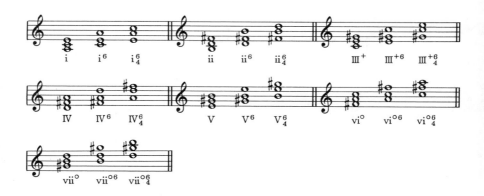

Note:

1. The raised seventh note ("si"-leading tone) in the harmonic minor scale results in three chord changes;

   III+ = augmented rather than major;
   V   = major rather than minor;
   vii° = diminished rather than major.

2. The raised sixth ("fi") and seventh notes ("si") in the ascending form of the melodic minor scale change the size of six chords:

   ii   = minor rather than diminished;
   III+ = augmented rather than major;

IV   = major rather than minor;
V   = major rather than minor;
vi°   = diminished rather than major;
vii° = diminished rather than major.

3. All changes are the result of chromatic alterations made on the original chords found in the natural minor form.

4. The descending melodic minor will be the same form as the natural minor.

Exercises

1. Write the three positions of each chord in all major keys.
2. Write the three positions of each chord in all natural minor keys.
3. Write the three positions of each chord in all harmonic minor keys.
4. Write the three positions of each chord in all ascending and descending melodic minor keys.

In each measure locate the root and then identify with the correct Roman and Arabic numerals the position of the triads which follow:

Major Keys

5. C Major

6. G Major

7. F Major

8 D Major

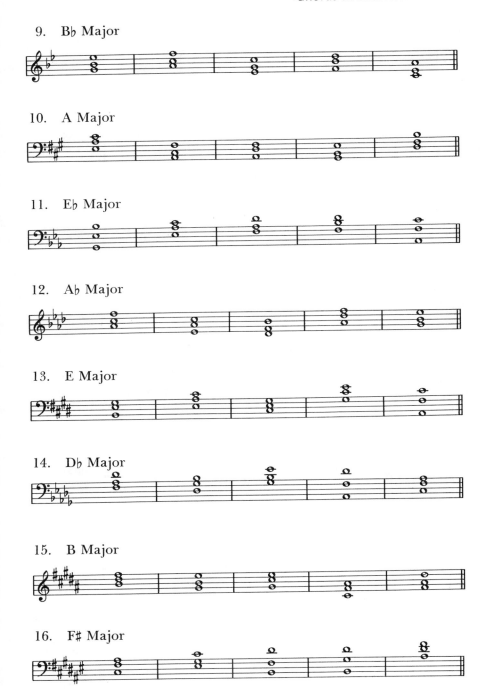

17. G♭ Major

18. C♭ Major

19. C♯ Major

Minor Keys

20. A minor

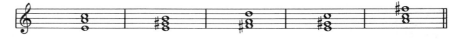

21. E minor

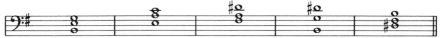

22. D minor

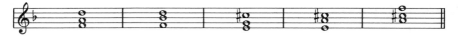

23. G minor

24.   B minor

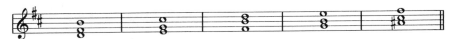

25.   F♯ minor

26.   C minor

27.   F minor

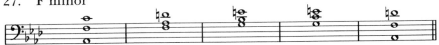

28.   B♭ minor

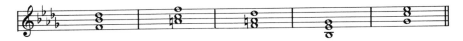

29.   C♯ minor

30.   G♯ minor

31. E♭ minor

32. A♭ minor

33. D♯ minor

34. A♯ minor

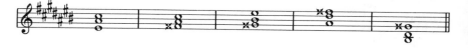

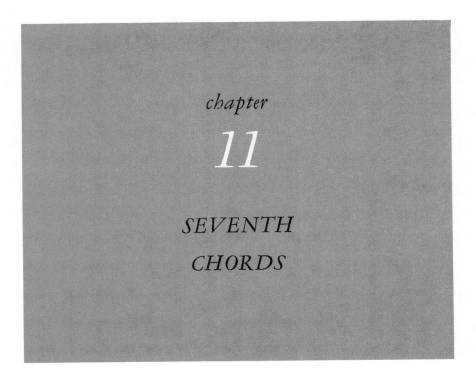

chapter

11

SEVENTH

CHORDS

CHARACTERISTICS OF THE SEVENTH CHORD

Seventh chords are four-note chords. The term *seventh* is used to show the addition of another interval of a third on top of a basic triad. It also indicates that the interval from the root (in root position) up to the added or highest note is the interval of a seventh. Seventh chords are dissonant chords because of the dissonance created between the root and the added seventh.

Major Seventh

Note:

1. Major third is on the bottom.
2. Minor third is in the middle.
3. Major third is on the top.

Seventh chords may be *major* as in the example above, or *minor:*

Minor Seventh

Root Position

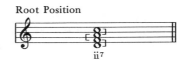

Note:

1. Minor third is on the bottom.
2. Major third is in the middle.
3. Minor third is on the top.

Seventh chords may be augmented:

Augmented Seventh

Root Position

Note:

1. Major third is on the bottom.
2. Major third is in the middle.
3. Minor third is on top.
4. Plus sign ($+$) indicates an augmented chord.
5. The augmented seventh chord is basically an augmented triad with an added seventh.

Seventh chords may be diminished:

Diminished Seventh

Root Position

iii°⁷

Note:

1. Minor third is on the bottom.
2. Minor third is in the middle.
3. Minor third is on the top.
4. Small zero indicates diminished chord.
5. Diminished seventh chords contain only intervals of a minor third.

Seventh chords may be half-diminished:

Half-Diminished Seventh

Root Position

iiiø⁷

Note:

1. Minor third is on the bottom.
2. Minor third is in the middle.
3. Major third is on the top.
4. Small zero slashed indicates half-diminished chord.

Seventh Chords on "C" Major Scale

I⁷   ii⁷   iii⁷   IV⁷   V⁷   vi⁷   vii°⁷   I

Note: Arrows in viiø⁷ indicate pull toward tonic chord. However, the vii°
is usually found in one of its inversions.

Seventh Chords on "a" Minor Scale—Natural

Seventh Chords on "a" Minor—Harmonic Form

Note: The raised seventh step in this scale will change the quality of some of the chords.

Seventh Chords on "a" Minor—Melodic Form

Ascending

Descending

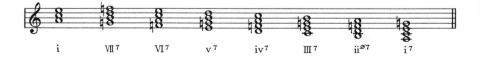

Note: The raised sixth and seventh degrees in the ascending form will change the quality of some of the chords.

DOMINANT SEVENTH CHORDS—ROOT POSITION

A seventh chord is in root position when the scale tone upon which it is based is on the bottom of the chord.

Root Position—Key of "C" Major

Seventh Chord

The seventh chords pictured above have minor seventh intervals between the root and seventh. This can be checked on the piano keyboard. Remember, a *minor seventh* interval represents a total of ten half steps between a given root and the minor seventh above this root.

Observe that the first example above is written as a minor seventh chord and is not capitalized because the lowest interval of a third ("re/fa") is a minor third. The second example is capitalized because of the major third ("sol/ti") on the bottom of the chord. The lower third determines major or minor in root position.

Although we have learned that seventh chords may be major, minor, augmented, or diminished and may be constructed on any note of the scale, we will now concentrate on an additional form of the seventh chord called the *dominant seventh chord*. This chord has the fifth tone of the scale ("sol" in major; "mi" in minor) for a root. The fifth tone of the scale is called *dominant*—hence, dominant seventh chord. The triad based on the fifth degree of the scale is likewise called a dominant triad.

The tonic in major ("do" or 1) or the tonic in minor ("la" or 1) is the central or principal note. The tonic chord is so called since it is based on the first note of the scale, which is called the tonic. The tonic chord is the principal chord in any key, major or minor.

The dominant chord based on "sol" (5) is the second most important chord in any key. The dominant scale tone ("sol" or 5) is called dominant because of its strong position in a melody and its pull toward the tonic. There is a polar attraction between the tonic and the dominant and vice versa. The tonic moves toward the dominant in a melody and the dominant then progresses toward the conclusion found in the tonic.

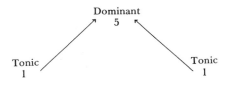

Dominant
5

Tonic
1

Tonic
1

This relationship between the tonic triad and the dominant triad is strong because of the presence of the leading tone ("ti" in major; "si" in minor) in the dominant triad. Since the leading tone is strongly attracted to "do" in major keys and "sol" also moves toward the tonic, we find the dominant triad focuses attention on the ultimate goal—the tonic. Likewise in minor, the leading tone "si" moves strongly toward "la," while "mi," the dominant tone in the minor scale, also moves to the tonic "la."

Dominant—Tonic

If we add a seventh to the dominant triad, we make this relationship even stronger, for we add "fa" to the dominant triad, which is strongly attracted toward "mi" in the tonic triad.

Note: The dominant seventh chords in root position in major keys have:

1. A major third interval on the bottom.
2. A minor third interval in the middle.
3. A minor third interval on top.
4. A dominant seventh chord in major built on "sol" (5) of the major scale.

Dominant Seventh Chord—Root Position

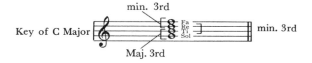

The tone ("fa") added to the basic dominant triad is strongly attracted to "mi" and thereby completes the attraction toward the tonic chord.

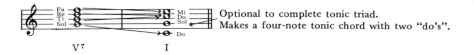

Note:

1. The V stands for dominant triad.
2. The Arabic 7 means the added note is seven scale steps above the root ("sol") of the dominant triad in major keys.

The dominant seventh chord in root position in minor keys has:

Natural Minor
Dominant Seventh

Not capitalized since bottom third is minor.
"Mi" is the fifth in minor scales.
"Re" is the seventh above "mi" in minor.

Harmonic Minor
Dominant Seventh

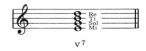

Capitalized since the lower third is major.
"Mi" is the fifth.
"Re" is the seventh above "mi" in minor.

Melodic Minor
Ascending
Dominant Seventh

Capitalized since major third is on bottom.
"Mi" is the fifth.
"Re" is the seventh above "mi" in minor.

Melodic Minor
Descending
Dominant Seventh

Not capitalized because of minor third on bottom.
"Mi" is the fifth.
"Re" is the seventh above "mi" in minor.

Note:

1. The V7 chord is identical in the harmonic minor and the melodic minor, ascending.
2. The v7 chord in melodic minor, descending form, is identical with the natural form.

Dominant Seventh to Tonic

"a" Natural Minor

"a" Harmonic Minor

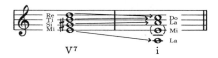

Note:

1. The seventh ("re") descends to "do."
2. This resolution causes the fifth ("mi") to be omitted in the tonic chord.
3. The fifth of any chord may be omitted with no loss of identity for the chord.

"a" Melodic Minor (Ascending)

"a" Melodic Minor (Descending)

Note:

1. "Sol" is not a leading tone in the descending form of the melodic minor scale.
2. The seventh ("re") descends to "do," thereby eliminating the fifth ("mi") in the tonic chord.
3. The lack of a leading tone ("si") in the natural minor weakens the pull toward the tonic ("la").
4. "Ti" pulls toward "do" in each instance; this establishes a feeling for the relative major, which has the same key signature as the minor.
5. Remember, the key name found one and one half steps above "la" will be the key signature for both the major key and its relative minor key.

6. All relative minors may be found through this process. (One and one half steps below the major keynote "do" will be the relative minor keynote "la.")

DOMINANT SEVENTH CHORDS—INVERSIONS

The dominant seventh chord is based on the fifth tone of the scale ("sol") in any major key. In minor keys, it is based on the fifth tone of the minor scale, which is "mi." The scale tone upon which a chord is based is the root. The triad, having three chord tones, has three positions: root position, first inversion, and second inversion. The dominant seventh chord, which has four tones, will have four positions. These are root position, first inversion, second inversion, and third inversion.

In the key of "C" Major the dominant seventh chord is based on G, which is "sol" in this key.

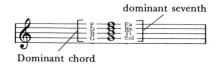

	C	D	E	F	G	A	B	C
	1	2	3	4	5	6	7	8
	do	re	mi	fa	sol	la	ti	do

In root position, the dominant chord in the key of "C" is built in intervals of a third with G ("sol") as the root.

Key of "C" Major

dominant seventh

F — Fa
D — Re
B — Ti
G — Sol

Dominant chord

The first three notes G B D ("sol-ti-re") represent the dominant triad,
V
which we have learned is second in importance to the tonic triad ("do-mi-sol" or C E G in the key of "C").
I
The complete four-note G B D F ("sol-ti-re-fa") is the dominant
V7
seventh chord in root position in the key of "C" Major. Notice the size of the intervals of this dominant chord in root position.

Chords in root position may result in angular or awkward chord progressions. For this reason, we resort to the inversions of a chord which can produce more movement and fluidity in a series of chord progressions.

The dominant seventh chord is particularly effective in the inversions because of the tendency tones ("ti" and "fa") contained in this chord. The following progressions of the dominant seventh chord (V7) to the tonic chord (I) show the typical movement of the individual tones in this progression.

Root Position

$$V^7 \qquad I$$

First Inversion

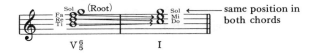

same position in both chords

$$V_5^6 \qquad I$$

Note:

1. V_5 .
2. V = Dominant.
3. 6 = Interval of a sixth between lowest ("ti") and highest ("sol").
4. 5 = Interval of a fifth between lowest ("ti") and second highest ("fa").
   Actually, the Arabic 6 will always indicate that the lowest note of any chord will be the third of the chord.

Natural Minor

$$v_5^6 \qquad i$$

Note:

1. Sol-la: The lack of a raised leading tone creates an elusive effect.
2. Ti-$\boxed{\text{do}}$: Relative major keynote.
3. Mi-mi: Common tone.
4. $\boxed{\text{Re}}$-do: Seventh of the chord.

Harmonic Minor

$$V_5^6 \qquad i$$

Note:

1. |Si|-la: Raised leading tone.
2. Ti-|do| : Relative major keynote.
3. Mi-mi: Common tone.
4. |Re|-do: Seventh of the chord.

Melodic Minor

Note:

1. |Si|-la: Raised leading tone.
2. Ti-|do| : Relative major keynote.
3. Mi-mi: Common tone.
4. |Re|-do: Seventh of the chord.

Second Inversion

Root keeps same position in both chords

Note:

1. V_3^4.
2. V = Dominant.
3. 4 = Interval of a fourth between the lowest note and the root of the chord.
4. 3 = Interval of a third between the lowest note and the next note of the chord.
5. Actually, this chord could be ennumerated $V_3^6{}_4$, which indicates that 6 = an interval of a sixth above the lowest note.

6. The interval between the lowest note and the root is a fourth.
7. The interval between the lowest note and the next note of the chord is a third.
8. The V will always indicate that a dominant chord is in second inversion with "re" as the lowest note.
9. "Re" is the fifth of a dominant chord in major and may be omitted without any loss of the chord identity.

Natural Minor

V_3^4 i^6 or i

Note:

1. Sol-la: No raised leading tone.
2. Ti- $\boxed{do}$: Relative major keynote $= i6$
or
   Ti-la: Tonic minor keynote $= i$.
3. Mi-mi: Common tone.
4. $\boxed{Re}$ -do: Seventh of the chord.

Harmonic Minor

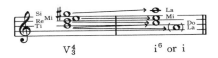

V_3^4 i^6 or i

Note:

1. $\boxed{Si}$ -la: Raised leading tone.
2. Ti- $\boxed{do}$: Relative major keynote $= i6$
or
   Ti- $\boxed{la}$: Tonic minor keynote $= i$.
3. Mi-mi: Common tone.
4. $\boxed{Re}$ -do: Seventh of the chord.

Melodic Minor

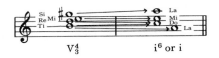

V_3^4 i^6 or i

Note:

1. Si -la: Raised leading tone.
2. Ti- do : Relative major keynote = i6
   or
   Ti-la: Tonic minor keynote = i.
3. Mi-mi: Common tone.
4. Re -do: Seventh of the chord.

Third Inversion

C Major

V²   I

Root keeps same position
in both chords

Note:

1. V² is an abbreviation for V$\frac{6}{4}{2}$.
2. Fa up to re is a sixth.
3. Fa up to ti is a fourth.
4. Fa up to sol is a second.
5. Since the distinguishing feature of this chord is the dissonant interval of a second (fa/sol), it is generally abbreviated V². Sometimes it appears as V$\frac{4}{2}$ which means the same as V².

Natural Minor

v²   i⁶

Note:

1. Sol-la: No raised leading tone.
2. Ti- do : Relative major keynote.
3. Mi-mi: Common tone.
4. Re -do: Seventh of the chord.

Harmonic Minor

Note:

1. Si -la: Raised leading tone.
2. Ti- do : Relative major keynote.
    or
   Ti- la : Tonic minor keynote.
3. Mi-mi: Common tone.
4. Re -do: Seventh of the chord.

Melodic Minor

Note:

1. Si -la: Raised leading tone.
2. Ti- do : Relative major keynote.
    or
   Ti- la : Tonic minor keynote.
3. Mi-mi: Common tone.
4. Re -do: Seventh of the chord.

FIGURED BASS

1. Chords in root position will be indicated by Roman numerals without any added Arabic numerals. In this textbook on theory and in some other theory texts, the major chords have capitalized Roman numerals while minor chords are not capitalized. Some texts do not differentiate and use capitalized Roman numerals throughout for both major and minor chords. Added Arabic numerals are implied

(5/3) but not written for root position. The 5/3 refers to the interval above the root (5 = fifth; 3 = third). The 5/3 indicates a chord in root position.

2. The first inversion of triads will be indicated through the addition of an Arabic numeral 6, which indicates that there is an interval of a sixth between the lowest note shown and the highest.

The other two intervals are not notated with Arabic numerals but are a fourth (4) and a third (3).

3. The second inversions are notated as

Both intervals are notated to avoid confusion with the first inversion.

4. Four-note seventh chords in root position and inversions are shown as

C Major

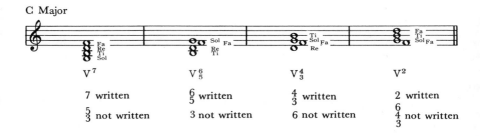

5. A chromatic sign (♯, ♭, or ♮) written independently of any Arabic numeral indicates that the third is to be altered. No Arabic numeral is necessary for the third.

6. All intervals other than the third require the addition of an Arabic numeral as well as a chromatic sign to show which interval is involved. The chromatic may be found in front of the Arabic numeral or behind it.

7. A line drawn through an Arabic numeral indicates that this note will be raised one half step.

8. A horizontal line indicates that the upper notes are to be held while the bass may move.

9. Arabic numerals which follow each other in succession are sometimes used to indicate a special feature such as a suspension or some other dissonant effect.

Exercises

In the following dominant to tonic progressions the dominant seventh chord is given. Complete the exercises by:

1. Supplying the tonic chord with tendency tones resolving correctly.
2. Writing the Latin syllables next to each note in the dominant seventh and tonic chords.
3. Giving the name of the key signature in each case.

Dominant Seventh to Tonic

Major

V^7 I V^6_5 I

V^4_3 I^6 V^2 I^6

V^7 I V^6_5 I

V^4_3 I^6 V^2 I^6

V^7 I V^6_5 I

Dominant Seventh to Tonic

Minor

GLOSSARY

MUSICAL TERMS

a cappella   unaccompanied choral music
accelerando   gradually faster
acoustics   the science of sound
adagietto   at a tempo slightly faster than adagio
adagio   indicating a slow tempo; not as slow as largo
ad libitum   a variance from strict tempo, determined by performer
affettuoso   tenderly
affrettando   hurrying
agitato   in excited, agitated manner
air   song, melody
alla   in the style of
allargando   slowing down
allegretto   faster than andante but slower than allegro
allegro   at a fast tempo
allegro vivace   fast, with life
all'ottava   at the octave

andante   moderately slow (walking tempo)

andantino   slightly faster than andante

animato   in an animated manner

a piacere   at the performer's discretion

appoggiatura   an accented nonharmonic tone

arpeggio   single chord tones played in succession

assai   very

a tempo   indicating a return to regular tempo

atonal, atonality   having no central key

bass   lowest male voice; lowest and largest of instruments

beam (ligature)   horizontal line connecting flags on notes

bitonal, bitonality   occurring in two different keys at the same time

brio   spirit, vigor

cadence   musical punctuation through formulas expressing a temporary pause or final conclusion

cadenza   a solo section for the display of a performer's. technique

calando   gradually diminishing

canon   strict imitation

cantabile   in a singing style

chanson   French word for song

chord   three or more tones sounding together

circle of fifths   a device used to indicate upper and lower dominants (keys five steps above or below a previous key)

comodo   at a comfortable tempo

con   with

con fuoco   with fire

consonance   a quality of music that is relatively at rest and pleasant-sounding

deciso   decisively, boldly

diatonic   relating to a scale having five whole tones and two semitones (half steps): do re \mi fa/ sol la \ti do/
                                              ½ step   ½ step

diminuendo   decreasing in loudness

dissonance   restless energy; relatively harsh sound

dolce   sweetly, tenderly

dolente   dolefully

dominant   fifth tone in a major or minor scale

doppio   double

duplet   two notes sounded in the same time space as three notes
dynamics   degree of energy or volume

enharmonic   relating to a tone or tones that are equivalent but written differently
espressivo   expressively

fugue   imitative counterpoint derived from short melody (subject) and imitated in other voices

gebrauchsmusik   music for amateurs
giocoso   joyously
giusto   in strict tempo
glissando   rapid sliding movement using thumb on piano keys
grace note   a musical ornament represented by a note in small type
grave   solemnly
grazioso   gracefully

harmonics   partial tones (overtones) sounding above a fundamental (strongest) tone
harmony   the vertical structure which results when tones are sounded together (chord)
homophony   one melody supported by harmony

improvisation   an invention form usually derived from a given melody
incalzando   hurrying
interval   the distance or measurement in pitch between two tones
intesso tempo   tempo in which the beat value remains the same
intonation   the condition of being in tune
inversion   reverse order of an interval; the upper tone becomes the lower tone

key   generally means the central tone of a scale or composition; also refers to the parts of an instrument manipulated by the performer's fingers
key signature   the sharps or flats at the beginning of a staff indicating the central tone to which other tones are related

largamente   broadly
larghetto   a little faster than largo
largo   at a very slow tempo
legato   in a smooth flowing style of connecting individual tones
leger (ledger)   lines above and below the staff
leggiero, leggero   lightly
leitmotiv   musical motive
lento   slowly
libretto   the text of an opera
l'istesso tempo   at the same tempo

maestoso   majestically
malinconico   in a melancholy manner
marcato   marked, with stress
marcia   march
melody   a meaningful succession of tones arranged in a horizontal
  manner
meno   less
meno moto   with less motion
mesto   sadly
meter   the pattern of fixed beats with primary and secondary
  accents
metronome   a mechanical device which gives the beat at adjust-
  able speeds
mezzo   half
mezzo forte (mf)   moderately loud
mezzo piano (mp)   moderately soft
minuet, menuetto   French dance in $\frac{3}{4}$ meter
moderato   moderately
modulation   change of key within a section
molto   very
monophony   single melodic line without accompaniment
morendo   fading away
mosso   in an agitated manner
motive   a melodic or rhythmic figure that unifies a composition

octave   the distance of eight tones between the lowest and highest
  notes of a diatonic scale
ostinato   a much repeated phrase or motive (relates to the word
  "obstinate")
ottava   octave

pedal point   a long-held note in the bass over which the harmony changes *usually* in the bass

pesante   in a heavy manner

pitch   a musical sound determined by the frequency of vibrations per second

piu   more

piu mosso   with more motion

poco   little

polyphony   two or more melodies existing simultaneously, independent of each other, yet complementing each other

polyrhythm   cross rhythms produced by the use of conflicting accents and meters

polytonal, polytonality   relating to two or more keys existing simultaneously

prestissimo   very fast

presto   fast

rallentando (rall.)   gradually slowing down

rhythm   the organized motion of music involving primary and secondary accents

ritardando (rit., ritard.)   growing slower

ritenuto   indicating a sudden reduction of tempo

round   a form of imitation

rubato   indicating a free interpretation of tempo left to the discretion of the performer

scherzando   playfully

segue   without a break or in the same manner

semitone   half step

semplice   in simple style

sempre   always

senza   without

sequence   a repetition of a motive generally at another pitch

sforzando (sfz.)   sudden accent followed by piano (soft)

sostenuto   in a sustained manner

sotto   under

subito   suddenly

suite   a collection of dance tunes

suspension   a nonharmonic tone which has been prepared as a consonance and is usually resolved by scale step

syncopation   a displacement of the normal accent

tempo   the speed of a composition

teneramente   tenderly

tenuto   in a sustained emphasized manner

timbre   tone color

time signature (meter)   the two figures or numbers which come after the key signature indicating the unit of beat and the number of beats per measure

tonality   music having a key center or central tone to which all other tones are related

tone   a musical sound having regular vibrations per second resulting in a pitch

tonic   the keynote

tranquillo   in tranquil manner, quietly

transpose   to place in another key

transposition   performing same melody and harmony at a different pitch level (key)

triad   a three-note chord

trill   a rapid alternation of two adjacent notes

triplet   three notes which are grouped together and are equal in value; an irregular division of the beat

troppo   too

una corde   soft pedal (left) of the piano; single string

vivace   in lively style, quickly

vivo   fast

MUSICAL SYMBOLS

accent   mark indicating stress on some notes

arpeggio   chord tones played singly in succession rather than together

bar lines   vertical lines separating measures

chromatics (accidentals)
    sharp ♯   raises a note one half step (semitone)
    flat ♭   lowers a note one half step (semitone)
    cancel (natural) ♮   removes the effect of a previous sharp or
    flat
    double sharp ♯♯ or ✗   raises a note two half steps
    double flat ♭♭   lowers a note two half steps

clefs
    alto clef (C clef)   indicates position of middle C

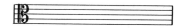

    bass clef (F clef) and staff   for low voices and instruments

    treble clef (G clef) and staff   for high voices and instruments

crescendo ◁───   gradually getting louder
decrescendo (diminuendo) ───▷   gradually getting
    softer

    double whole note |𝅝| or   ‖𝅝‖   a note having twice the
    value of the whole note o

fermata   hold

grand staff   staff combining highest to lowest tones

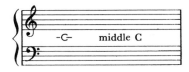

hammer stroke   a heavy form of staccato

leger (ledger) lines   lines above or below a staff

musical alphabet   A-B-C-D-E-F-G-A-B-C-D-E-F-G

octave sign   8ᵛᵉ (8ᵛᵃ)   sign indicating a sound one octave above the written note

repeat signs

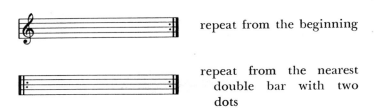

repeat from the beginning

repeat from the nearest double bar with two dots

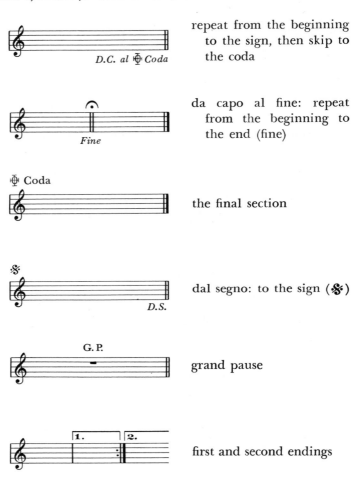

repeat from the beginning to the sign, then skip to the coda

da capo al fine: repeat from the beginning to the end (fine)

the final section

dal segno: to the sign (𝄋)

grand pause

first and second endings

rest

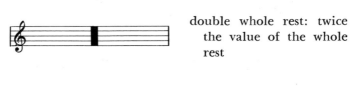

double whole rest: twice the value of the whole rest

multiple measures of rest are indicated by a numeral above the rest

slur   notes on different lines and spaces which are connected in legato style

staccato   dots indicating a short and detached style

staccato slurred   slurred, yet articulated within the slur

stop   //   an abrupt stop

tenuto   in a sustained emphasized manner

tie   a curved line connecting notes on the same line or space, making one long tone for the total number of beats represented

trill   rapid repetition of two adjacent notes

tr ∿∿∿∿∿∿∿∿∿∿

INDEX

Detach starting from
upper lefthand margin.

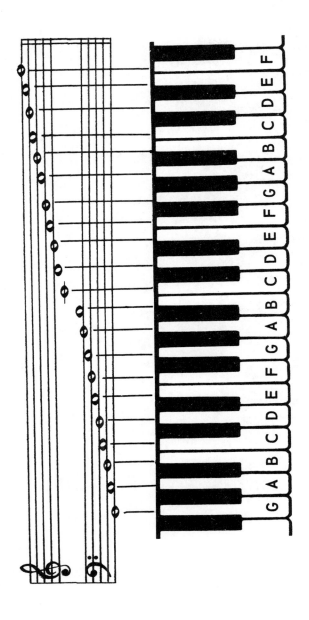